PATCHWORK
STYLE

PATCHWORK STYLE

· · · · ·

35 SIMPLE PROJECTS
FOR A COZY & COLORFUL LIFE

Suzuko Koseki

TRUMPETER
Boston & London
2009

CONTENTS

INTRODUCTION

There are two kinds of patchwork items: the kind that can take you hours of painstaking hand-piecing, and the kind that you can make quickly and easily with a sewing machine. Either one can be extremely attractive.

In this book, I will show you how much fun it can be to make patchwork items with a sewing machine. Enjoyment is what I had in mind as I created each of these projects.

—SUZUKO KOSEKI

CHANGE PURSES

Even those little scraps of fabric that you have been throwing away can be sewn together to create unexpectedly attractive items. This pouch has a special clasp that pops open when you press both sides. INSTRUCTIONS ON PAGES 60 AND 63.

LOG CABIN

Machine stitching scraps of fabric together makes it easy to create log cabin squares. You don't need a pattern. Just sew the pieces together one by one, starting in the middle, and you'll gradually create a cohesive piece of fabric.

MINIBAG

You create this small bag by taking a single piece of log cabin quilting and folding it in half. The addition of a gusset gives the bag form and changes the look of the patchwork pattern, which makes it more fun.

INSTRUCTIONS ON PAGE 64.

QUILT

This coverlet is made up of thirty large log cabin squares. I used contrasting fabrics in the center and outer frame of each square and two color patterns throughout the entire quilt. You can complete even a major project like this one quickly and easily by using a sewing machine.

INSTRUCTIONS ON PAGE 67.

PILLOW COVER

I made this pillow cover with a red and black color scheme. It took me a long time to figure out the proper balance of solids, stripes, and prints, but once I found the right composition, I was able to sew up the final piece in no time at all.

INSTRUCTIONS ON PAGE 69.

RED BAG

I decorated this chic red bag with black daisies and folded the raw edges of the flower petals under to create a cleaner look.

INSTRUCTIONS ON PAGE 71.

APPLIQUÉ

Many of the standard appliqué patterns—and probably some of the first to come to mind—are flower motifs. The projects in this section give you some straightforward methods for securing appliqués and finishing items with machine stitching.

BLACK BAG

Because of the strong contrast between the black background and the white daisies, you need to be careful of the appliqué placement. You should also consider how the pattern will look when you carry it over your shoulder.

INSTRUCTIONS ON PAGE 75.

BAG WITH A METAL FRAME

I inserted a large metal frame to hold the shape of the bag opening. The appliqués are laid on the foundation cloth as they are cut out and are fixed in place with free motion stitching.

INSTRUCTIONS ON PAGE 77.

FLOWERED BAG

This bag is a fun play on the homophones flower and flour: The fabric is an old-fashioned flour sack, and I appliquéd lots of flowers all over this bag. I also attached two types of handles.

INSTRUCTIONS ON PAGE 81.

NET 50 POUNDS
CONTRACT NO. MP (FF) 22.679 KILO
USE NO HOOKS
22266
CAPE WEST BANK

CHANGE PURSE

I appliquéd a leaf pattern onto this smaller zippered purse because it's more interesting to use different motifs for the main bag and change purse instead of trying to match them. The contrasting striped fabric adds extra visual impact.

INSTRUCTIONS ON PAGE 85.

COASTER,
PLACE MAT,
AND TRAY

I used actual leaves as the patterns for these appliqué pieces, and with a little backing and free stitching, they stand out in relief. The table settings are designed to be reversible, so you can use different fabrics for each side.

INSTRUCTIONS ON PAGE 87.

PATCHWORK SQUARES

After sewing strips of fabric together, you can employ the common method of machine piecing—cutting them horizontally and sewing them together—or quilt the strips together.

MINIBAG

This design is based on a small paper bag. A sewing machine allows you to do the detailed work quickly and easily. Can you find something else in this book that uses the same combination of colors?

INSTRUCTIONS ON PAGE 91.

TOTE BAG

I put this bag together from a variety of red, blue, and white prints. If you're new to machine piecing, this kind of project is a good place to start. Here, I made a gusset by pinching and pulling out the bottom corners. I decided to leave the corners flat rather than attach them to the seam.

INSTRUCTIONS ON PAGE 93.

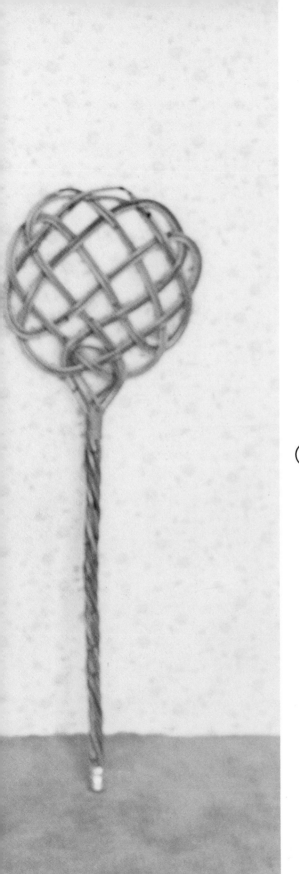

LAP QUILT

I used wool for the back and borders of this blanket, which is just the right size to use as a lap quilt. I finished it by laying rickrack over the seams, so it doesn't matter if they're not precise.

INSTRUCTIONS ON PAGE 95.

FAN-SHAPED BAG

Strips of fabric remnants are sewn directly onto quilt batting and lining material. By sewing the strips together as you quilt, you can finish this bag in no time

INSTRUCTIONS ON PAGE 97.

POCKET TISSUE CASE

To make this case, I started with an elegant purple print and attached well-coordinated strips of lace. Inside are slots for two packs of tissues.

INSTRUCTIONS ON PAGE 99.

FAN-SHAPED MINIBAG

I used different designs on the front and back of this little bag, which has the odd effect of making it seem either longer than it is tall or taller than it is long, depending on which side you're looking at. If you like, you can use whichever design you prefer on both sides.

INSTRUCTIONS ON PAGE 101.

RED PARTY BAG

The impression created by ragged fabric remnants is one of wonderful softness and flexibility. For this bag, I tore up some old red kimono fabric and made it into a ruffle. You can adjust the strap to any length you wish.

INSTRUCTIONS ON PAGE 103.

BLUE PARTY BAG

Even though it has the same design as the purse on the facing page, using different materials makes this bag look completely different. It also has a shorter handle and would even look cute hanging off the handle of a larger bag.

INSTRUCTIONS ON PAGE 103.

SHOULDER BAG

This is a great bag for holding little odds and ends or for keeping your valuables close at hand when you take a walk. You can either run a belt through it and wear it around your waist or attach a shoulder strap and make it into a small shoulder bag.

INSTRUCTIONS ON PAGE 107.

38

PILLOW COVER

Here, I simply took patchwork pieces and sewed them around a big red square. This pillow cover would also look great if the square were made of a large-patterned print instead of a solid color.

INSTRUCTIONS ON PAGE 110.

QUILT

I made this quilt by taking pieces of fabric that were all the same width and cutting them to different lengths. I then sewed the pieces into the rows to make the quilt top. Repeated laundering only improves the texture of this quilt.

INSTRUCTIONS ON PAGE 112.

FREE STITCHING

Most modern sewing machines have a free motion function that lets you use them for embroidery. Give free rein to your imagination as you use straight and zigzag stitches to decorate your creations.

POCKET TISSUE CASE

Free motion stitching will seem difficult until you get used to it, but once you're able to move the fabric around as you please, you'll enjoy it so much you won't want to stop. Of course, it's best to start by making small items, such as these pocket tissue cases.

INSTRUCTIONS ON PAGE 115.

PILLOW COVER

For this project I embroidered the Roman numerals by machine. The pattern was inspired by some of my favorite prints, as were those used for the lap quilt on the opposite page. The two dominant colors are yellow and black.

INSTRUCTIONS ON PAGE 117.

LAP QUILT

I had some of my favorite yellow print fabric left over, but there wasn't enough to make a whole item, so I combined it with other fabric remnants. I came up with a design that used one of my favorite color combinations: yellow, black, and white.
INSTRUCTIONS ON PAGE 119.

POT HOLDERS

It feels more natural to use the same pot holders for a long time, but now I can't bring myself to get rid of these! If you're going to use an item every day, you might as well have fun making it.

INSTRUCTIONS ON PAGE 121.

SQUARE APPLIQUÉ

As the name implies, this technique uses square pieces of fabric. Trim the squares neatly, then lay them out on your main fabric with the seam allowances tucked under—or you can allow the raw edges to show. Make up a tidy arrangement of horizontal and vertical pieces, or arrange them randomly. It's up to you.

SHOULDER BAG

If you take freshly cut, untrimmed squares, put them on your fabric, and machine quilt them with tiny stitches, you'll end up with what looks like a single piece of fabric. Changing the color of the machine thread occasionally lets you provide color accents. INSTRUCTIONS ON PAGE 124.

CURTAIN

Take a simple lattice-patterned curtain and appliqué your favorite fabrics on to give it an instant makeover. I chose the placement of the appliqué squares while the curtain hung in the window so I could get a better sense of the overall balance.
INSTRUCTIONS ON PAGE 127.

TOTE BAG

After embroidering the lattice lines on the bag with your sewing machine, lay different colored fabrics in the squares. Be sure to leave a few squares empty here and there. Keep the back simple, with just a single flower to decorate it.

INSTRUCTIONS ON PAGE 128.

FOLDED POT HOLDERS

You usually use pot holders folded any-
way, right? Well, these are made to be
folded over from the beginning.

INSTRUCTIONS ON PAGE 131.

POT HOLDERS

These rectangular pot holders are the typical kind. They give you an opportunity to use up fabric remnants, no matter how small, and your friends will appreciate receiving them as gifts.

INSTRUCTIONS ON PAGE 133.

POCKET TISSUE CASE

You can pull your tissues out through the slot in this zippered pouch. Appliqué an assortment of fabrics onto the linen surface in a well-balanced arrangement. The red zipper is a nice extra touch
INSTRUCTIONS ON PAGE 136.

APRON

This front-tie apron has a lot of pockets, which makes it convenient for cooking or quilting. Use it to store your glasses, scissors, thimbles, rulers, and any other small items that tend to go missing.

INSTRUCTIONS ON PAGE 138.

FLOOR MAT

Kitchen floor mats tend to become soiled easily, but if this mat gets dirty, you can just sew more layers on top. It's fun to see how the design gradually changes as the mat is used.

INSTRUCTIONS ON PAGE 140.

HOW TO MAKE

A NOTE ON THE PROJECTS

Only finished measurements are provided for most of the projects in this book. Please read through all of the instructions carefully before preparing your materials. Be sure to add a seam allowance to the finished dimensions before cutting your fabric. Patchwork piecing is commonly given a seam allowance of ¼", while simple hems are usually given a ⅜" allowance.

CHANGE PURSE WITHOUT STRAP

Photograph on page 8 (purse on the right)

MATERIALS

- Fabric scraps for patchwork (prints, solids, stripes, checks; the colors and patterns are up to you)
- Top band (print or solid): 6" × 6"
- Lining (cotton): 12" × 6"
- Quilt batting: 18" × 6"
- Internal flex frame (1): 4" wide

FINISHED MEASUREMENTS

Add all seam allowances before cutting your fabric. *See Figure 1.*

INSTRUCTIONS

1. Using your fabric scraps, make two log cabins approximately 12" × 6" for the purse front and back, following the instructions on page 61.

2. Place each log cabin, right side up, on the quilt batting. Machine quilt the fabric and batting together, making rows about ¼" apart. Mark the finished shape of the pouch on the fabric and cut around it, leaving a seam allowance. *See Figure 2.*

3. Lay each of the top band pieces, right side up, on the quilt batting. Machine quilt the fabric and batting together, making rows about ¼" apart. Place the right sides of two band pieces together and stitch along the short sides. Turn the band right side out and stitch close to the edge along the seams. Fold the band in half lengthwise and baste the long edges together. Repeat for the second band. *See Figure 3.*

4. Align the long raw edge of a top band with the top edge of the purse front, right sides together. Stitch in place. Repeat for the purse back. Place the purse front and back right sides together and stitch around the bottom and both sides. *See Figure 4.*

5. Place both pieces of lining fabric right sides together and sew around the bottom and both sides, making sure the lining has the same dimensions as the purse. Turn the lining right side out and place it over the purse, wrong sides together. Fold the top edge of the lining to the wrong side and hand stitch the edge to the top bands. Turn the pouch right side out. *See Figure 5.*

6. Remove one of the hinges on the flex frame, pull the frame through the openings in the top bands, and replace the hinge to secure. *See Figure 5.*

HOW TO SEW A LOG CABIN

To make a log cabin, start with a piece of fabric in any size you choose (piece 1). Take a second piece of fabric (piece 2) and lay it on piece 1, right sides together. Align one edge and stitch. Open and trim any excess fabric. Place a third piece of fabric on pieces 1 and 2, right sides together. Align the one edge of piece 3 against the joined pieces and stitch. Open and trim if necessary. Continue stitching pieces together in this manner until you've created a piece of fabric in the desired size.

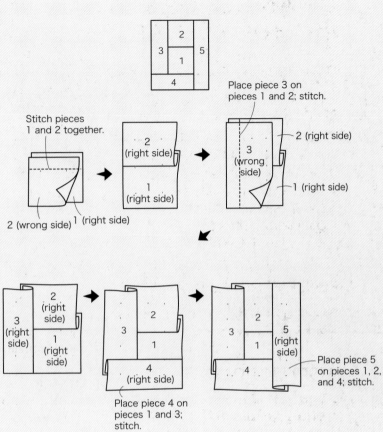

FIGURE 1

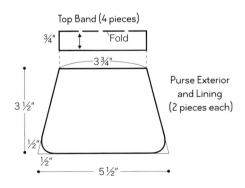

Top Band (4 pieces)

¾"   Fold

3 ¾"

3 ½"

½"

½"

5 ½"

Purse Exterior and Lining (2 pieces each)

FIGURE 2

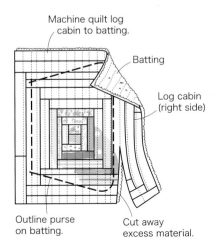

Machine quilt log cabin to batting.

Batting

Log cabin (right side)

Outline purse on batting.

Cut away excess material.

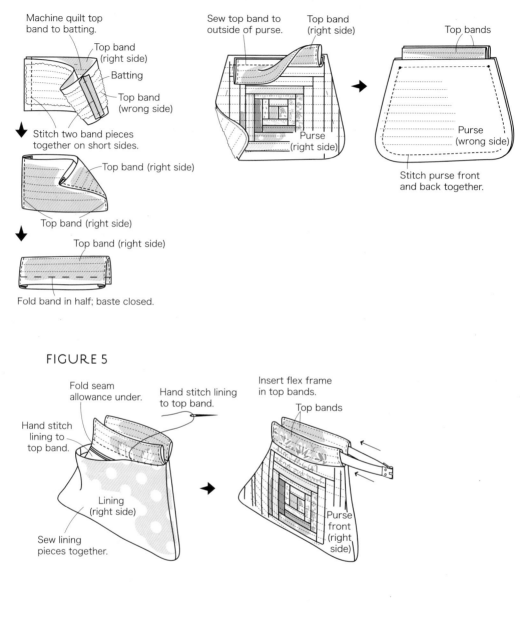

FIGURE 3

Machine quilt top band to batting.

Top band (right side)

Batting

Top band (wrong side)

Stitch two band pieces together on short sides.

Top band (right side)

Top band (right side)

Top band (right side)

Fold band in half; baste closed.

FIGURE 4

Sew top band to outside of purse.

Top band (right side)

Top bands

Purse (right side)

Purse (wrong side)

Stitch purse front and back together.

FIGURE 5

Fold seam allowance under.

Hand stitch lining to top band.

Hand stitch lining to top band.

Insert flex frame in top bands.

Top bands

Lining (right side)

Sew lining pieces together.

Purse front (right side)

CHANGE PURSE WITH STRAP

Photograph on page 8 (purse on the left)

MATERIALS

- Fabric scraps for patchwork (prints, solids, checks, polka dots; the colors and patterns are up to you)
- Top band (solid color): 6" × 10"
- Lining (cotton): 12" × 6"
- Quilt batting: 18" × 6"
- Cord for strap: 12" long × ¼" wide
- Internal flex frame (1): 4" wide

FINISHED MEASUREMENTS

Add all seam allowances before cutting your fabric. *See Figure 1.*

INSTRUCTIONS

1. Follow steps 1 through 4 for the Change Purse without Strap on page 60.

2. Place the ends of the cord on the purse side seams, aligning the ends with the bottom edge of the top band; stitch in place. Place both pieces of lining fabric right sides together and sew around the bottom and both sides, making sure the lining has the same dimensions as the purse. Turn the lining right side out and place it over the purse, wrong sides together. Fold the top edge of the lining to the wrong side and hand stitch the edge to the top bands, covering the ends of the cord. Turn the purse right side out. *See Figure 2.*

3. Remove one of the hinges on the flex frame, pull the frame through the opening in the top bands, and replace the hinge to secure.

FIGURE 1

Top Band (4 pieces)

Purse Exterior and Lining (2 pieces each)

Fold ↕ ¾"

3¾"

1⅛"

2⅜"

½"

½"

5½"

FIGURE 2

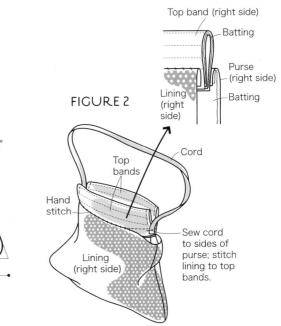

Top band (right side)

Batting

Purse (right side)

Lining (right side)

Batting

Cord

Top bands

Hand stitch

Sew cord to sides of purse; stitch lining to top bands.

Lining (right side)

MINIBAG

Photograph on page 10

MATERIALS

- Fabric scraps for patchwork (prints, stripes, solids; the colors and patterns are up to you)
- Decorative patch (1)
- Fabric for gussets, handle, and lining (solid): 35" × 15¾"
- Bias tape (double fold): ¼" × 21"
- Backing (lightweight cotton): 12" × 10"
- Quilt batting: 15¾" × 15¾"
- Zipper (1): 11½" long
- Pompom (1): ½" in diameter

FINISHED MEASUREMENTS

Add all seam allowances before cutting your fabric. *See Figure 1.*

INSTRUCTIONS

1. Place the zipper right side up on the right side of the top gusset lining and baste it in place. Lay the top gusset exterior over the zipper, wrong side up, and place a piece of batting cut to the same size on top of this. Align raw edges and stitch along one side of the zipper, making sure to go through all layers. Fold the gusset fabric and batting away from the zipper and machine quilt the layers together, making rows ¼" apart. Repeat with the second top gusset on the other side of the zipper.

2. Place the bottom gusset exterior on the bottom gusset lining, right sides together. Place one end of the top gusset between the layers, with the right sides of the exterior pieces together. Place the batting on the wrong side of the bottom gusset exterior. Stitch along one side, being sure to sew through all layers. Fold the bottom gusset fabric and batting away from the top gusset and machine quilt the layers together, making rows ¼" apart. Repeat with the second bottom gusset on the opposite side of the top gusset. *See Figure 2.*

3. Follow the instructions on page 61 to make one log cabin approximately 8½" × 9¼".

4. Place the log cabin right side up on the batting and the cotton backing. Machine quilt the pieces together, making rows about ¼" apart. Machine stitch the decorative patch to the log cabin surface. Mark the finished shape of the bag on the fabric and cut around it, leaving a seam allowance. *See Figure 3.*

5. Start with a piece of fabric 2" × 7½" for each handle. Fold each long edge to the center of the wrong side twice, then fold the handle in half lengthwise and edgestitch. Each finished handle will be ¼" wide. *See Figure 4.*

6. Follow the instructions on page 70 to make the pocket. Sew the pocket to the right side of the lining. Place the lining and bag exterior wrong sides together and baste in place. Baste the handles to the right sides of the bag exterior, keeping in mind that the finished length of each handle should be 6¾". *See Figure 5.*

7. Align the bag exterior and gusset with right sides together. Stitch in place, leaving a seam allowance. *See Figure 6.*

8. Fold the bias tape over the seams. Fold the seam toward the bag lining, and hand stitch the bias tape and seam to the lining. Turn the bag right side out and sew the pompom to the zipper tab. *See Figure 7.*

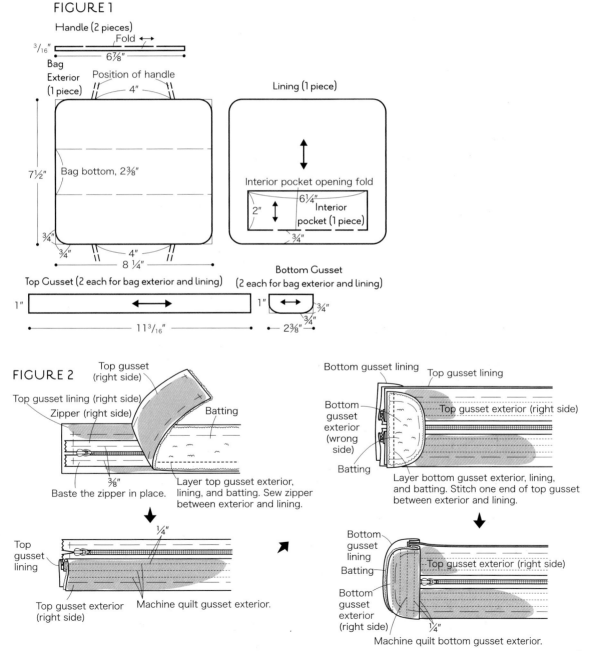

FIGURE 1

Handle (2 pieces)
Fold
3/16"
6⅞"

Bag Exterior (1 piece)
Position of handle
4"
7½"
Bag bottom, 2⅜"
¾"
¾"
4"
8 ¼"

Lining (1 piece)
Interior pocket opening fold
6¼"
2"
Interior pocket (1 piece)
¾"

Top Gusset (2 each for bag exterior and lining)
1"
11³/₁₆"

Bottom Gusset (2 each for bag exterior and lining)
1"
¾"
¾"
2⅜"

FIGURE 2

Top gusset (right side)
Top gusset lining (right side)
Zipper (right side)
Batting
⅜"
Baste the zipper in place.
Layer top gusset exterior, lining, and batting. Sew zipper between exterior and lining.

Top gusset lining
¼"
Top gusset exterior (right side)
Machine quilt gusset exterior.

Bottom gusset lining
Top gusset lining
Bottom gusset exterior (wrong side)
Top gusset exterior (right side)
Batting
Layer bottom gusset exterior, lining, and batting. Stitch one end of top gusset between exterior and lining.

Bottom gusset lining
Batting
Top gusset exterior (right side)
Bottom gusset exterior (right side)
¼"
Machine quilt bottom gusset exterior.

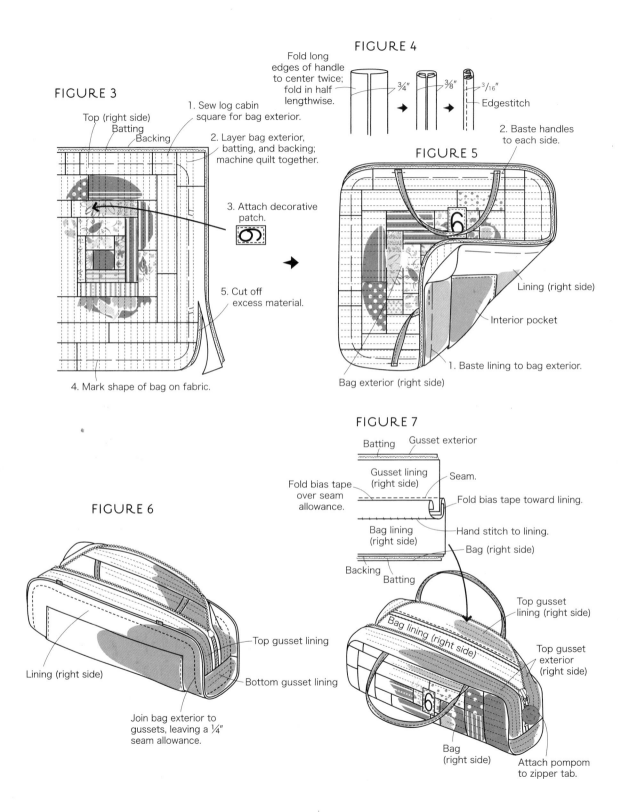

FIGURE 3

Top (right side)
Batting
Backing

1. Sew log cabin square for bag exterior.

2. Layer bag exterior, batting, and backing; machine quilt together.

3. Attach decorative patch.

5. Cut off excess material.

4. Mark shape of bag on fabric.

FIGURE 4

Fold long edges of handle to center twice; fold in half lengthwise.

¾"   ⅜"   3/16"

Edgestitch

2. Baste handles to each side.

FIGURE 5

Lining (right side)

Interior pocket

1. Baste lining to bag exterior.

Bag exterior (right side)

FIGURE 6

Lining (right side)

Top gusset lining

Bottom gusset lining

Join bag exterior to gussets, leaving a ¼" seam allowance.

FIGURE 7

Batting   Gusset exterior

Gusset lining (right side)

Seam.

Fold bias tape over seam allowance.

Fold bias tape toward lining.

Bag lining (right side)

Hand stitch to lining.

Bag (right side)

Backing   Batting

Bag lining (right side)

Top gusset lining (right side)

Top gusset exterior (right side)

Bag (right side)

Attach pompom to zipper tab.

QUILT

Photograph on page 12

MATERIALS

- Fabric scraps for patchwork (prints, solids, stripes, checks; the colors and patterns are up to you)
- Fabric for binding (cotton): 35½" × 47¼"
- Back (cotton): 35½" × 168"
- Quilt batting: 51" × 157½"
- Worsted weight yarn (the colors are up to you)

FINISHED MEASUREMENTS

Add all seam allowances before cutting your fabric. *See Figure 1.*

INSTRUCTIONS

1. Mark the size of the finished square—13¾ × 13¾"—on the batting. Also mark an interior frame—7" × 7"—centered in the first square, to indicate when to switch color schemes. Place your first piece of fabric (piece A) on the batting, in the center of the square, and machine quilt it, making rows ¼" apart. Place your next piece of fabric (piece B)—of whatever width you like—on piece A, right sides together. Align the right edges and stitch in place. Fold piece B back over the batting and machine quilt. Continue in this manner, adding fabric to the log cabin and machine quilting, until you've sewn beyond the finished square size. Mark the finished dimensions again and cut around it, leaving a seam allowance. Make a total of 30 squares: 15 with a dark-colored outer frame and light-colored inner square, and 15 squares with a light-colored frame and dark-colored inner square. *See Figure 2.*

2. Lay out the squares in an arrangement you like, with 5 squares in each row and alternating the light and dark squares. Sew the squares together in 6 rows, pressing the seam allowances open as you go, then sew the rows together.

3. Lay the quilt top on the back, wrong sides together. Baste or pin the layers in place, then machine quilt them together along the seams, outlining the squares. *See Figure 3.*

4. Tie the quilt in 99 places, placing a tie in the center of each square and in the center of each square seam. To make a tie, insert one strand of yarn in the quilt top ⅛" from the point of the tie center, leaving a tail approximately 2" long. Pull the yarn out ⅛" from the tie center on the opposite side from where the yarn entered, and cut a tail approximately 2" long. Repeat on the other two sides of the tie center. Tie the two strands of yarn to the left of the

tie center together and the two strands to the right of the tie center together close to the quilt top. Tie all four loose ends together twice over the tie center. Trim the ends. To prevent the knots from loosening, apply an antifraying liquid or hobby glue. *See Figure 4.*

5. Sew the binding around the edge of the quilt, following the instructions on page 114.

page 114

FIGURE 1

Quilt Top Finished quilt top measures 69¾" × 83½". Binding measures ⅜".   • indicates positions of ties.

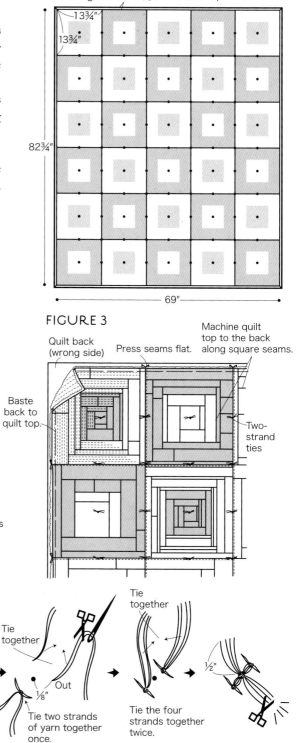

13¾"
13¾"
82¾"
69"

FIGURE 2

Mark finished square size and color-change frame on batting.

Place center fabric (A) on batting and machine quilt.

Place pieces B–F in order around piece A; stitch in place and machine quilt each.

Mark final dimensions again; cut away excess material.

15¾"
7"
E
F
D   A   B
C
7"
Batting
40

FIGURE 3

Quilt back (wrong side)   Press seams flat.

Machine quilt top to the back along square seams.

Baste back to quilt top.

Two-strand ties

FIGURE 4

In
⅛"
Center

⅛"
Out

In
⅛"

Tie together
⅛"
Out
Tie two strands of yarn together once.

Tie together
Tie the four strands together twice.

½"

PILLOW COVER

Photograph on page 13

MATERIALS

- Fabric scraps for patchwork (prints, solids, lace; the patterns and colors are up to you)
- Backing fabric (thin cotton) (2): 15¾" × 15¾"
- Pillow back fabric (cotton striped): 31½" × 15¾"
- Quilt batting: 15¾" × 15¾"
- Bias tape (double fold): ¼" × 59"
- Decorative patch (1)
- Zipper (1): 11¾" long

FINISHED MEASUREMENTS

Add all seam allowances before cutting your fabric. *See Figure 1.*

INSTRUCTIONS

1. Baste the batting to the backing fabric. Place the first piece of fabric (piece A) on the batting and pin it in place. Arrange pieces B through F (the width of each is up to you) around piece A. To sew, place each piece face down, one at a time in order, and stitch. Add lace to the patchwork as you desire. *See Figure 2.*

2. Mark the finished dimensions on the fabric and cut around it, leaving a seam allowance. Machine quilt all three layers—the backing, batting, and log cabin—together, making rows ⅜" apart. Sew on the decorative patch. Lay the pillow top on the second piece of backing fabric, right side up, and baste. *See Figure 3.*

3. Place the two panels for the pillow back right sides together, aligning one long edge. Baste the panels together and press the seam open. Fold the seam allowance ⅛" toward the wrong sides. Align the zipper with the fold line on one side and stitch in place. Open the fabric and top-stitch the zipper in place. Remove the basting thread. *See Figure 4.*

4. Lay the pillow back on the pillow top, right sides together. Stitch around all four sides. Open up the bias tape and place on the pillow case, aligning raw edges. Stitch in the fold of the bias tape. Fold the bias tape over the seam allowance, and hand stitch in place. Open the zipper to turn the pillow cover right side out. *See Figure 5.*

FIGURE 1

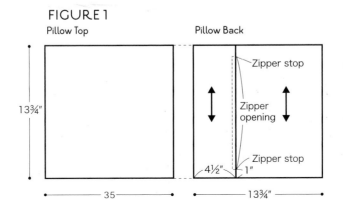

Pillow Top — 13¾" — 35

Pillow Back — Zipper stop — Zipper opening — Zipper stop — 4½" — 1" — 13¾"

FIGURE 2

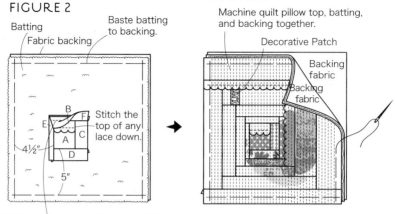

Batting
Fabric backing
Baste batting to backing.

B
E F
A C
D
4½"
5"

Stitch the top of any lace down.

Pin fabric pieces to batting and stitch.

FIGURE 3

Machine quilt pillow top, batting, and backing together.

Decorative Patch

Backing fabric

Backing fabric

FIGURE 4

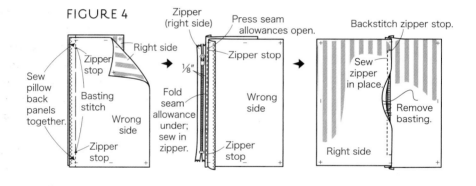

Sew pillow back panels together.

Zipper stop
Right side
Basting stitch
Wrong side
Zipper stop

Zipper (right side)
Press seam allowances open.
Zipper stop
⅛"
Fold seam allowance under; sew in zipper.
Wrong side
Zipper stop

Backstitch zipper stop.
Sew zipper in place.
Remove basting.
Right side

FIGURE 5

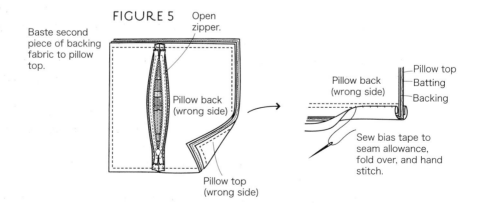

Baste second piece of backing fabric to pillow top.

Open zipper.

Pillow back (wrong side)

Pillow top (wrong side)

Pillow back (wrong side)

Pillow top
Batting
Backing

Sew bias tape to seam allowance, fold over, and hand stitch.

RED BAG

Photograph on page 16

MATERIALS

- Fabric scraps for appliqués (solids, prints, dots; the colors and patterns are up to you)
- Fabric for bag front (red cotton): 23⅝" × 17¾"
- Fabric for bag back and handle loops (red cotton): 23⅝" × 21⅝"
- Lining (lightweight cotton): 23⅝" × 17¾"
- Quilt batting: 23⅝" × 17¾"
- Fusible interfacing: 35½" × 15¾"
- Button (1): ¾" in diameter
- Ready-made leather handles (2): ⅓" wide × 19¾" long; or leather straps (2): ⅓" wide × 19¾" long with 4 D-rings and 4 cap rivets

FINISHED MEASUREMENTS

Add all seam allowances before cutting your fabric. *See Figure 1.*

INSTRUCTIONS

1. Lay the bag front, right side up, on the batting and backing. Machine quilt all three layers together, starting at the bottom of the bag and stopping 2½" from the top edge, making the rows ¼" apart. Mark the finished shape of the bag and the dart lines on the fabric and machine baste ¼" around the inside edge of the outline; cut around the outline, leaving a seam allowance. Pinch the fabric for the darts on the wrong side; align and then sew along the marked lines. Press the seam allowance toward the bag center. Repeat for the bag back, machine quilting in rows ¼" apart and stopping ¾" from the top edge.

   Sew on the appliqué (following the instructions on page 73). Attach all the petals, making sure to keep the composition balanced. Hand stitch the button to the appliqué in the center of the flower.

   Place the bag front on the bag back, right sides together, and stitch around the bottom and both sides. *See Figure 2.*

2. Adhere fusible interfacing to the pocket fabric according to the manufacturer's instructions. Fold the pocket fabric in half, right sides together. Stitch along the bottom and two sides, leaving a 2¾" gap on the bottom. Turn the pocket right side out. Fold the raw edges of the gap toward the wrong side and press.

   Adhere fusible interfacing to the wrong side of the lining front and back according to the manufacturer's directions. Place the pocket on the right side of the lining back. Stitch in place along the sides and bottom, then down the pocket center, dividing the pocket in two. Pinch the fabric for the darts on the wrong side, aligning and then sewing along the marked lines. Press the seam allowance toward the bag center. Place the lining front and back right sides together. Stitch along three sides, leaving a 5½" opening along the bottom. *See Figure 3.*

3. Take a piece of fabric 1" × 6" to be used for attaching the handles; fold the long edges toward the center, then fold

the fabric in half. Stitch along both long sides, then cut the strip into four pieces, each 1½" long. If using ready-made handles, loop each fabric pieces through the end of each handle; if using leather straps, loop each fabric piece through a D-ring.

Place the fabric loops on the right side of the bag exterior where the ends of the handles will be. The loops extend just beyond the top edge; baste in place making sure the front and back D-rings are aligned. Turn the bag right side out. Place the bag inside the lining with right sides together. Sew along the top edge, being sure to sew through the fabric loops. Turn the bag right side out through the opening in the lining. Hand stitch the opening closed. *See Figure 4.*

4. If you're using leather straps, pass the ends of the leather straps through the D-rings. Fold the ends against the strap, ¾" from the D-ring. Punch a hole through both layers, and secure in place with a cap rivet. *See Figure 5.*

FIGURE 1

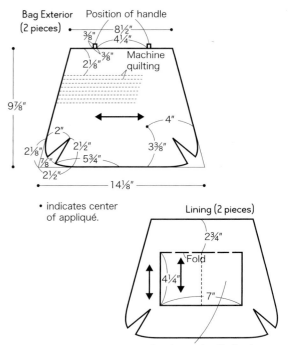

• indicates center of appliqué.

FIGURE 2

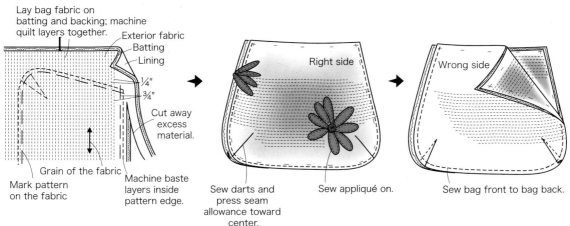

HOW TO APPLIQUÉ

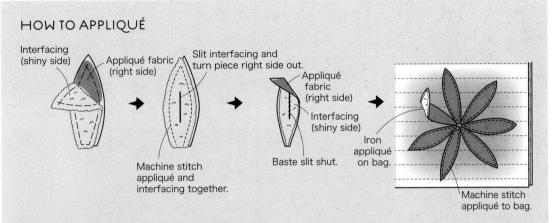

Interfacing (shiny side)

Appliqué fabric (right side)

Slit interfacing and turn piece right side out.

Appliqué fabric (right side)

Interfacing (shiny side)

Iron appliqué on bag.

Machine stitch appliqué and interfacing together.

Baste slit shut.

Machine stitch appliqué to bag.

Using the template (see page 74) as a guide, cut out appliqué pieces from the fabric and the fusible interfacing. Place the shiny side of the interfacing on the right side of the fabric and machine stitch the layers together around all sides. Cut a slit in the interfacing, being careful not to cut the fabric, and turn the piece right side out. Baste the slit closed. Place the appliqué piece on your project and iron it in place according to the manufacturer's directions. Machine stitch around each appliqué piece to secure in it place.

FIGURE 3

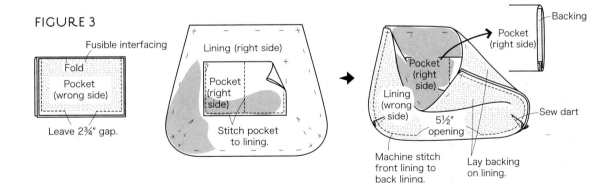

Fusible interfacing

Fold

Pocket (wrong side)

Leave 2¾" gap.

Lining (right side)

Pocket (right side)

Stitch pocket to lining.

Backing

Pocket (right side)

Pocket (right side)

Lining (wrong side)

5½" opening

Sew dart

Machine stitch front lining to back lining.

Lay backing on lining.

FIGURE 4

Fold fabric strip lengthwise
twice toward center, stitch
sides, and cut in 4 pieces.

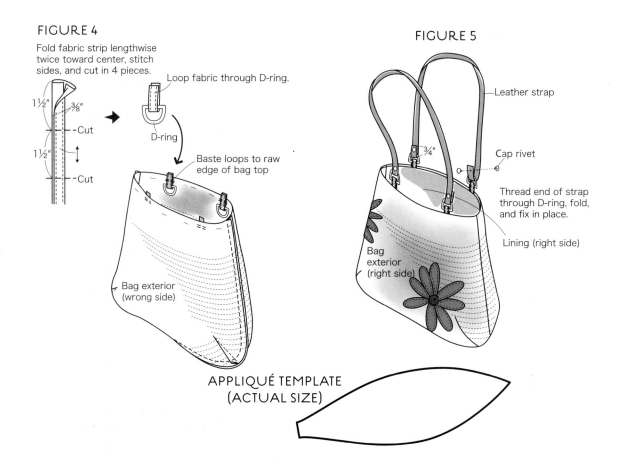

Loop fabric through D-ring.

1½" ⅜"

--Cut

1½"

--Cut

D-ring

Baste loops to raw
edge of bag top

Bag exterior
(wrong side)

FIGURE 5

Leather strap

¾"

Cap rivet

Thread end of strap
through D-ring, fold,
and fix in place.

Lining (right side)

Bag
exterior
(right side)

APPLIQUÉ TEMPLATE
(ACTUAL SIZE)

BLACK BAG

Photograph on pages 18–19

MATERIALS

- Fabric scraps for appliqués (cotton sheeting, cotton prints; the colors and patterns are up to you)
- Fabric for bag exterior (black cotton): $21\frac{5}{8}$" × $17\frac{3}{4}$"
- Lining (polyester satin): $23\frac{5}{8}$" × $21\frac{5}{8}$"
- Backing fabric (thin cotton): $21\frac{5}{8}$" × $17\frac{3}{4}$"
- Quilt batting: $21\frac{5}{8}$" × $17\frac{3}{4}$"
- Fusible interfacing for appliqués: 10" × 6"
- Fusible interfacing for lining: $23\frac{1}{2}$" × $19\frac{3}{4}$"
- Rickrack: $\frac{1}{2}$" wide × 59" long
- Buttons for flowers (3): $\frac{3}{4}$" in diameter
- Buttons to secure handle (2): $\frac{3}{4}$" in diameter
- Buttons to secure handle (2): $\frac{1}{4}$" in diameter
- Magnetic button (1): $\frac{3}{4}$" in diameter
- Ready-made handle (1): 27"

FINISHED MEASUREMENTS

Add all seam allowances before cutting your fabric. *See Figure 1.*

INSTRUCTIONS

1. Place the bag front fabric, right side up, on the batting and backing. Machine quilt all three layers together, starting at bottom of bag and stopping $\frac{3}{4}$" from the top edge, making the rows $\frac{1}{2}$" apart. Mark the finished shape of the bag and the dart lines on the fabric and baste $\frac{1}{4}$" around the inside edge of the outline; cut around the outline, leaving a seam allowance. Pinch the fabric for the darts on the wrong side; align and then sew along the marked lines. Press the seam allowance toward the center.

    Using the template on page 74, cut 7 petals for the top appliqué and 5 petals for the lower one. (You will also need 8 petals for the appliqué on the bag back.) Arrange the petals as shown in the photos on pages 18–19, and attach appliqués following the instructions on page 73. Sew a $\frac{3}{4}$" button at the center of each flower. Hand stitch the rickrack along the outside edge of the bag front; since the rickrack is wide, sew down the tops of the curves.

    Repeat for the bag back.

    Place the bag front on the bag back, right sides together. Stitch along the bottom and both sides; turn right side out. *See Figure 2.*

2. Create the interior pocket and lining following the instructions on page 71.

3. Place the bag lining over the exterior with right sides together. Machine stitch around the bag top; turn right side out. *See Figure 3.*

4. Attach the magnetic button following the instructions on page 101. Using thick thread, sew the buttons to the sides of the bag while also securing the ends of the handle. Place one end of the handle and one large button on the bag exterior; sew the button in place through handle, the bag, and then through the smaller button inside the bag, using the

smaller button as an anchor. Leave some space between the larger buttons and bag for the end of the handle to move. *See Figure 4.*

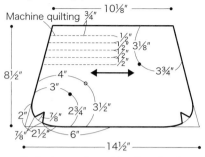

FIGURE 1

Bag Exterior (2 pieces)

Machine quilting ¾"

10⅛"

½"
½" 3⅛"
½"

3¾"

8½"

4"
3"

2" ⅞" 2¾" 3½"
⅞" 2½" 6"

14½"

•indicates centers of front appliqués;
○indicates center of back appliqué.

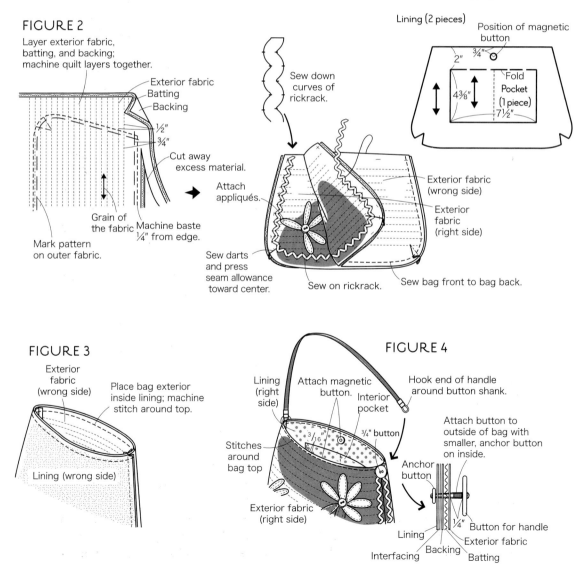

FIGURE 2

Layer exterior fabric, batting, and backing; machine quilt layers together.

Exterior fabric
Batting
Backing

½"
¾"

Cut away excess material.

Grain of the fabric

Machine baste ¼" from edge.

Mark pattern on outer fabric.

Sew down curves of rickrack.

Attach appliqués.

Sew darts and press seam allowance toward center.

Sew on rickrack.

Exterior fabric (wrong side)

Exterior fabric (right side)

Sew bag front to bag back.

Lining (2 pieces)

Position of magnetic button

2" ¾"

Fold

4⅜"

Pocket (1 piece)

7½"

FIGURE 3

Exterior fabric (wrong side)

Place bag exterior inside lining; machine stitch around top.

Lining (wrong side)

FIGURE 4

Lining (right side)

Attach magnetic button.

Interior pocket

Hook end of handle around button shank.

³/16" ¾" button

Stitches around bag top

Exterior fabric (right side)

Attach button to outside of bag with smaller, anchor button on inside.

Anchor button

¼"

Button for handle

Lining

Exterior fabric

Interfacing

Backing

Batting

76

BAG WITH A METAL FRAME

Photograph on page 20

MATERIALS

- Fabric scraps for appliqués (prints; the colors and patterns are up to you)
- Decorative lace flower (1)
- A bit of yarn (the color is up to you)
- Fabric for bag exterior (linen): 35½" × 13¾"
- Fabric for bag top and handle (cotton, solid color): 19¾" × 19¾"
- Fabric for lining (cotton): 35½" × 21½"
- Quilt batting: 35½" × 17¾"
- Double-sided fusible interfacing for appliqués: 17¾" × 9⅞"
- Fusible interfacing for lining and handles: 35½" × 21½"
- Bias tape (double fold): ¼" × 33"
- Metal tubular internal bag frame (1): 10" × 4"

FINISHED MEASUREMENTS

Add all seam allowances before cutting your fabric. *See Figure 1.*

INSTRUCTIONS

1. Lay the bag front, right side up, on the batting and baste in place. Using the measurements in Figure 1 and the templates on page 80 as a guide, cut out the appliqués; attach them to the bag following the directions on page 79 and sew on the lace flower. With your sewing machine set for free motion, create decorative stitching around the flowers. Make the center of the flower by pulling the yarn apart into strands, bunching them together, and fixing them in place with your sewing machine set for free motion. Sew around the letters and squares 3 to 5 times with a straight stitch. Repeat for bag back. *See Figure 2.*

2. Lay the fabric for the bag top on the bag front, right sides together; align the top edge and stitch in place. Fold the bag top up and machine quilt it to the batting, making rows ⅜" apart. Mark the finished shape of the bag on the fabric and cut around it, leaving a seam allowance. Repeat for the bag back. *See Figure 3.*

3. Lay the bag front on the bag back, right sides together, and stitch along the bottom and both sides. Leave an opening approximately 2" long centered along both side seams of the bag top; these will be used for inserting the metal rim. Form a gusset for the bag by flattening the bottom corners of the bag to a width of 3⅛". Stitch in place and cut off the corner, leaving a seam allowance. Turn bag right side out. *See Figure 4.*

4. Make the interior pocket and lining following the directions on page 71. *See Figure 5.*

5. Place the bag lining in the bag exterior, wrong sides together, and stitch the two layers together around the openings for the metal rim.

   Attach the fusible interfacing to the wrong side of the handle fabric according to the manufacturer's directions. To make each handle, fold both long edges toward the wrong side by ⅜" and press. Place a piece of batting, approximately

I³⁄₈" wide, on the wrong side of the handle; fold the handle fabric over the batting, aligning the folded edges. Machine quilt the handles together, making rows ³⁄₈" apart. Sew the handles in place on the right side of the bag top, aligning the raw edges of the handles with the bag top.

Open up the bias tape and place on the bag top, aligning raw edges. Stitch in the fold of the bias tape. Fold the bias tape over the bag top and leave the other side of the bias tape open. Fold the bag top in half toward the wrong side of the bag so the openings for the metal ring are at the top edge. Sew a concealed seam to attach the bag top and bias binding to the lining. Insert the metal frame by removing the joints from both ends; slide each half through a side opening and replace the joints. *See Figure 6.*

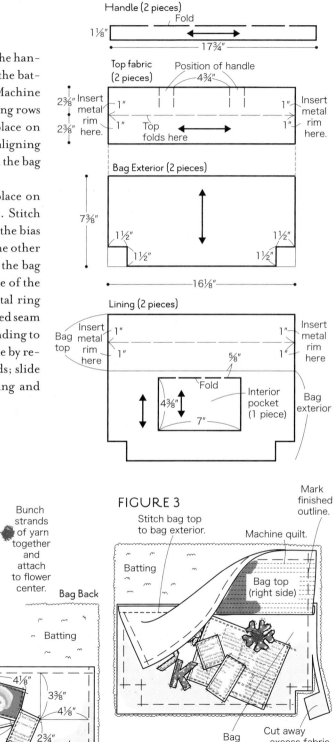

FIGURE 1

Handle (2 pieces)

Fold

1¹⁄₈"
17³⁄₄"

Top fabric (2 pieces)

Position of handle
4³⁄₄"

2³⁄₈" Insert metal rim here.
1"
1"
Top folds here

Insert metal rim here.
1"
1"

2³⁄₈"

Bag Exterior (2 pieces)

7³⁄₈"
1¹⁄₂"
1¹⁄₂"
1¹⁄₂"
1¹⁄₂"

16¹⁄₈"

Lining (2 pieces)

Bag top
Insert metal rim here
1"
1"

Insert metal rim here
1"
1"

Fold
5⁄₈"
4³⁄₈"
7"
Interior pocket (1 piece)
Bag exterior

FIGURE 2

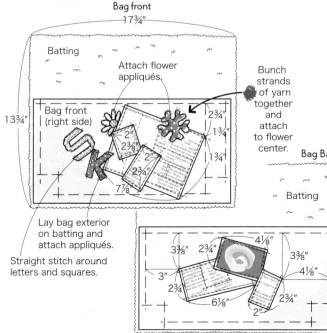

Bag front
17³⁄₄"

Batting

Attach flower appliqués.

Bunch strands of yarn together and attach to flower center.

13³⁄₄"
Bag front (right side)
2³⁄₄"
1³⁄₄"
2"
2³⁄₈"
2"
2³⁄₄"
1³⁄₄"
7⁷⁄₈"

Lay bag exterior on batting and attach appliqués.

Straight stitch around letters and squares.

Bag Back

Batting

3³⁄₈" 2³⁄₄"
4¹⁄₈"
3³⁄₈"
3"
4¹⁄₈"
2³⁄₄"
6¹⁄₈"
2"
2³⁄₄"

FIGURE 3

Stitch bag top to bag exterior.

Mark finished outline.

Machine quilt.

Batting

Bag top (right side)

Bag exterior (right side)

Cut away excess fabric.

78

HOW TO MAKE APPLIQUÉ LETTERS

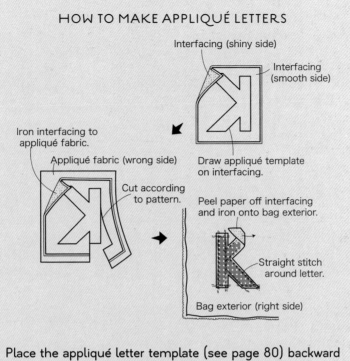

Interfacing (shiny side)

Interfacing (smooth side)

Iron interfacing to appliqué fabric.

Appliqué fabric (wrong side)

Draw appliqué template on interfacing.

Cut according to pattern.

Peel paper off interfacing and iron onto bag exterior.

Straight stitch around letter.

Bag exterior (right side)

Place the appliqué letter template (see page 80) backward on the smooth side of the double-sided interfacing and trace. Attach the interfacing to the wrong side of the appliqué fabric according to the manufacturer's directions. Cut out the letter, peel the paper off the interfacing, and attach the letter to the bag exterior according to the interfacing manufacturer's instructions. Straight stitch around the letter 3 to 5 times to secure it in place.

FIGURE 4

FIGURE 5

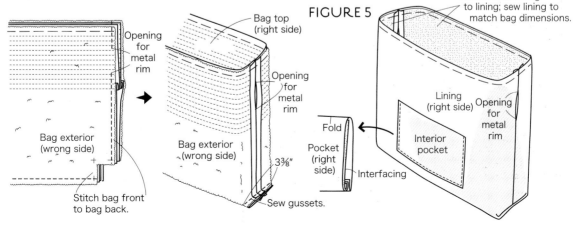

Opening for metal rim

Bag exterior (wrong side)

Stitch bag front to bag back.

Bag top (right side)

Opening for metal rim

Bag exterior (wrong side)

3⅜"

Sew gussets.

Attach interfacing to lining; sew lining to match bag dimensions.

Lining (right side)

Opening for metal rim

Fold

Pocket (right side)

Interior pocket

Interfacing

FIGURE 6

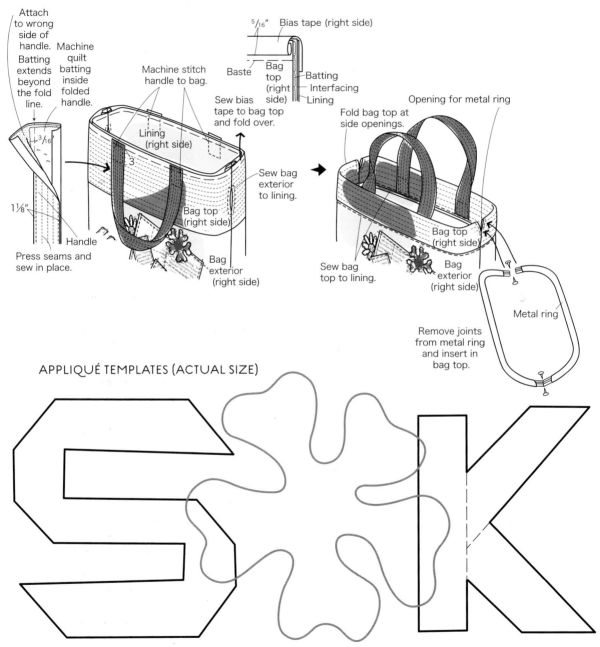

Attach to wrong side of handle. Batting extends beyond the fold line.

Machine quilt batting inside folded handle.

³⁄₁₆

1⅛"

Handle

Press seams and sew in place.

Machine stitch handle to bag.

Lining (right side)

3

Bag top (right side)

Bag exterior (right side)

⁵⁄₁₆" Bias tape (right side)

Baste

Bag top (right side)

Batting

Interfacing

Lining

Sew bias tape to bag top and fold over.

Sew bag exterior to lining.

Opening for metal ring

Fold bag top at side openings.

Sew bag top to lining.

Bag top (right side)

Bag exterior (right side)

Metal ring

Remove joints from metal ring and insert in bag top.

APPLIQUÉ TEMPLATES (ACTUAL SIZE)

FLOWERED BAG

Photograph on page 22

MATERIALS

- Fabric scraps for appliqués (prints, solids; the patterns and colors are up to you)
- Yarn, embroidery floss, or fabric scraps for the flower centers
- Fabric for bag exterior (wool): $25\frac{5}{8}$" × $15\frac{3}{4}$"
- Fabric for bag bottom and interior pocket (cotton sheeting): $29\frac{1}{2}$" × $11\frac{7}{8}$"
- Fabric for lining and tabs (print): $25\frac{5}{8}$" × $15\frac{3}{4}$"
- Fusible interfacing for appliqués: $15\frac{3}{4}$" × $11\frac{7}{8}$"
- Quilt batting: $25\frac{5}{8}$" × $15\frac{3}{4}$"
- Heavyweight fusible interfacing for bottom: $7\frac{7}{8}$" × $3\frac{1}{8}$"
- Leather strap: $\frac{3}{8}$" wide × $43\frac{1}{4}$" long, to be cut for three handles
- D-rings (2): $\frac{3}{4}$" in diameter
- Cap rivets (2): $\frac{1}{4}$" in diameter

FINISHED MEASUREMENTS

Add all seam allowances before cutting your fabric. *See Figure 1.*

INSTRUCTIONS

1. Lay the bag front on the batting and machine quilt the layers together, making rows $\frac{1}{4}$" apart.

    Using the templates on page 84, cut out the appliqué flowers. Use the diagram on page 82 to arrange the flowers on the bag exterior, then attach them following the instructions on page 79. Bunch up yarn, cloth scraps, and/or embroidery floss in the center of each flower and fix them in place by stitching around them in a spiral pattern using the free motion setting on your machine.

    Place the bottom fabric on the bag front, right sides together, and stitch in place. Fold the fabric down and attach more appliqué flowers so they overlap the bottom fabric. *See Figure 2.*

2. Sew the bag back in the same manner as the bag front, paying special attention to the placement of the flower appliqué that overlaps the back and bottom pieces. *See Figure 3.*

3. Place the bag front on the bag back, right sides together, and stitch along the bottom and both sides. Place a leather strap, 10" in length, along the top edge of the right side of the bag front, making sure the ends extend beyond the bag top, and baste it in place; repeat for the second handle on the bag back. (Note: The finished length of each handle should be $8\frac{1}{2}$".) *See Figure 4.*

4. Use two pieces of fabric, each $1\frac{1}{2}$" wide × 2" long, to make two tabs. For each tab, fold the long edges to the center, then fold the fabric in half; stitch along both long sides. Thread each tab through a D-ring; baste the tabs to the side seams of the bag.

    Form gussets by flattening the bottom corners of the bag to a width of $3\frac{1}{8}$". Stitch in place and cut off the corner, leaving a seam allowance. Adhere fusible interfacing, cut to approximately 7⅞" × 3⅛", to the bag bottom according to the manufacturer's directions. *See Figure 5.*

5. Make the interior pocket and lining following the instructions on page 71. Place the bag lining over the bag exterior, right sides together, and stitch around the bag top. Turn the bag right side out through the opening in the lining. Pass the ends of a leather strap 21⅝" long through the D-rings. Fold the ends against the strap, ¾" from the D-ring. Punch a hole through both layers, and secure in place with a cap rivet. *See Figure 6.*

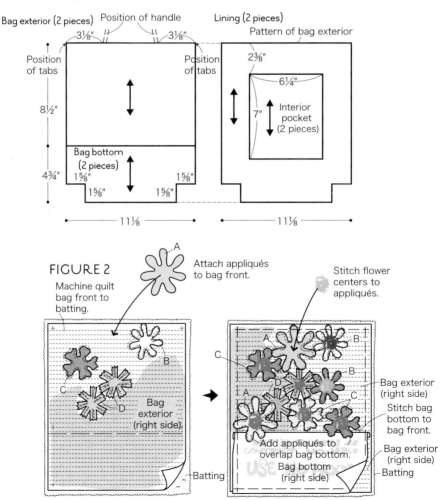

FIGURE 1

Bag exterior (2 pieces) Position of handle Lining (2 pieces)

3⅛"   3⅛"   Pattern of bag exterior

Position of tabs   Position of tabs   2⅜"

8½"   6¼"   7"   Interior pocket (2 pieces)

4¾" Bag bottom (2 pieces)

1⅝"   1⅝"
1⅝"   1⅝"

11⅛   11⅛

FIGURE 2

A Attach appliqués to bag front.

Machine quilt bag front to batting.

Stitch flower centers to appliqués.

Bag exterior (right side)

B
C
C
D

Bag exterior (right side)

Batting

A B
B
C
A D

Bag exterior (right side)
Stitch bag bottom to bag front.

Add appliqués to overlap bag bottom.
Bag bottom (right side)

Bag exterior (right side)
Batting

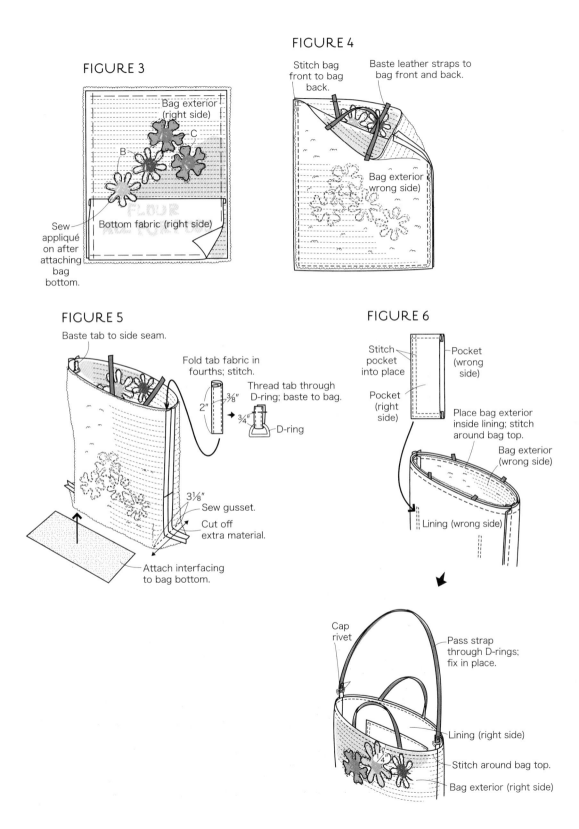

FIGURE 3

Bag exterior (right side)

C

B

Sew appliqué on after attaching bag bottom.

Bottom fabric (right side)

FIGURE 4

Stitch bag front to bag back.

Baste leather straps to bag front and back.

Bag exterior (wrong side)

FIGURE 5

Baste tab to side seam.

Fold tab fabric in fourths; stitch.

2"   ⅜"

Thread tab through D-ring; baste to bag.

¾"

D-ring

3⅛"

Sew gusset.

Cut off extra material.

Attach interfacing to bag bottom.

FIGURE 6

Stitch pocket into place

Pocket (wrong side)

Pocket (right side)

Place bag exterior inside lining; stitch around bag top.

Bag exterior (wrong side)

Lining (wrong side)

Cap rivet

Pass strap through D-rings; fix in place.

Lining (right side)

Stitch around bag top.

Bag exterior (right side)

APPLIQUÉ TEMPLATES
(ACTUAL SIZE)

For the Bag Front
A, B, D
(2 pieces each);
C (3 pieces)

For the Bag Back
B, C (2 pieces each)

Stitch around flowers
(pieces A, B, and C)
3 times, letting stitches
wander over the edges.

C

A

B

For back of change
purse (see instructions
on page 85)

Cut with pinking
sheers.

D

Machine stitch.

For front of purse
(see instructions on page 85)

CHANGE PURSE

Photograph on page 23

MATERIALS

- Fabric scraps for appliqué (velveteen; the amount and colors are up to you)
- Embroidery thread (the colors are up to you)
- Fabric for bag exterior (solid, cotton): $7\frac{7}{8}$" × 4"
- Contrasting fabrics for bag exterior (sheeting and stripes): 4" × 4"
- Lining (print): $15\frac{3}{4}$" × $5\frac{7}{8}$"
- Binding for top (velveteen): $5\frac{7}{8}$" × $5\frac{7}{8}$" or bias tape (double fold): $\frac{1}{4}$" × $5\frac{7}{8}$"
- Binding for sides (silk de chine): $5\frac{7}{8}$" × $5\frac{7}{8}$" or bias tape (double fold): $\frac{1}{4}$" × $5\frac{7}{8}$"
- Fusible interfacing: $5\frac{7}{8}$" × 4"
- Quilt batting: $15\frac{3}{4}$" × $5\frac{7}{8}$"
- Rickrack: $\frac{1}{4}$" wide × $31\frac{1}{2}$" long
- Zipper (1): $5\frac{1}{2}$" long

FINISHED MEASUREMENTS

Add all seam allowances before cutting your fabric. *See Figure 1.*

INSTRUCTIONS

1. Place the exterior fabric, right side up, on the batting; machine quilt the layers together, making rows $\frac{1}{4}$" apart. Use the templates on page 84 as guides to cut out appliqué pieces; attach them to the right side of the pouch exterior following the instructions on page 73. Create a seam allowance and cutaway the excess material. *See Figure 2.*

2. Lay the first contrasting exterior fabric on the purse front, right sides together, and align the raw edges. Stitch in place; open the fabric. Place the second contrasting fabric on the first, right sides together, and align the raw edges. Stitch in place; open the fabric. Machine quilt the contrasting fabrics to the purse front, making rows $\frac{1}{4}$" apart. Repeat for the purse back.

   Cut a strip of velveteen fabric $1\frac{3}{16}$" wide. Align the raw edge of the velveteen binding with the top edge of the purse front. Sew $\frac{1}{4}$" from the top edge and fold the binding over to the wrong side of the purse. Repeat for the purse back. *See Figure 3.*

3. Center the zipper horizontally along the top of the purse front. Align the teeth of the zipper against the binding; machine stitch it in place $\frac{1}{4}$" from the top edge, just below the binding on the purse front. Repeat with the other side of the zipper on the purse back.

   Cut the pouch lining for the bag front; place the lining on the purse front, wrong sides together. Fold the top edge of the lining toward the wrong side, and hand stitch the lining to the zipper tape. Mark and cut the finished shape of the purse. Repeat for the purse back. *See Figure 4.*

4. Place the purse front on the purse back, wrong sides together. Stitch along the bottom and both sides, close to the edge. Cut a piece of silk de chine $\frac{3}{4}$" wide; fold the long edges to the center. Align one folded edge of the binding

with the sides and bottom of the purse; stitch 3/16" from the edge. Fold the ends of the binding at the purse top down; fold the binding over to the purse back and hand stitch it in place. *See Figure 5.*

5. Hand stitch the rickrack to the purse front and back, covering the seam of the binding. *See Figure 6.*

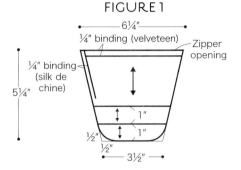

FIGURE 1

6¼"
¼" binding (velveteen)
Zipper opening
¼" binding (silk de chine)
5¼"
1"
1"
½"
½"
3½"

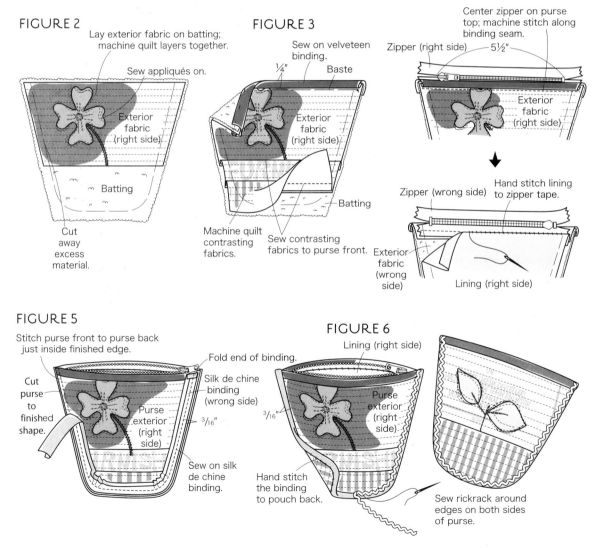

FIGURE 2

Lay exterior fabric on batting; machine quilt layers together.

Sew appliqués on.

Exterior fabric (right side)

Batting

Cut away excess material.

FIGURE 3

Sew on velveteen binding.

Baste

¼"

Exterior fabric (right side)

Batting

Machine quilt contrasting fabrics.

Sew contrasting fabrics to purse front.

FIGURE 4

Center zipper on purse top; machine stitch along binding seam.

Zipper (right side)
5½"

Exterior fabric (right side)

Zipper (wrong side)
Hand stitch lining to zipper tape.

Exterior fabric (wrong side)

Lining (right side)

FIGURE 5

Stitch purse front to purse back just inside finished edge.

Fold end of binding.

Cut purse to finished shape.

Silk de chine binding (wrong side)

Purse exterior (right side)

3/16"

Sew on silk de chine binding.

FIGURE 6

Lining (right side)

Purse exterior (right side)

3/16"

Hand stitch the binding to pouch back.

Sew rickrack around edges on both sides of purse.

COASTER, PLACE MAT, AND TRAY

Photograph on page 24

MATERIALS FOR THE COASTER (MAKES ONE)

- Fabric scraps for appliqués (prints, velveteen, jacquard; the patterns and colors are up to you)
- Fabric for top (cotton canvas): $5\frac{7}{8}$" × $5\frac{7}{8}$"
- Fabric for bottom (print): $11\frac{7}{8}$" × $5\frac{7}{8}$"
- Quilt batting: $7\frac{7}{8}$" × $5\frac{5}{8}$"

MATERIALS FOR THE PLACE MAT (MAKES ONE)

- Fabric scraps for appliqués (prints, velveteen; the patterns and colors are up to you)
- Fabric for top (cotton canvas): $19\frac{3}{4}$" × $13\frac{3}{4}$"
- Fabric for bottom (print): $19\frac{3}{4}$" × $13\frac{3}{4}$"
- Quilt batting: $19\frac{3}{4}$" × $13\frac{3}{4}$"

MATERIALS FOR THE TRAY

- Fabric scraps for appliqués (prints; the patterns and colors are up to you)
- Fabric for top (cotton canvas): $13\frac{3}{4}$" × $13\frac{3}{4}$"
- Fabric for bottom (print): $13\frac{3}{4}$" × $13\frac{3}{4}$"
- Quilt batting: $27\frac{1}{2}$" × $13\frac{3}{4}$"
- Heavyweight fusible interfacing: $11\frac{7}{8}$" × $11\frac{7}{8}$"
- Pompoms (4): $\frac{5}{8}$" in diameter

INSTRUCTIONS

1. To make the coaster, lay the coaster top, right side up, on the batting. Using the fabric scraps, sew a rectangular piece of fabric, in a size of your choosing, to the coaster top. Using the template on page 89 as a guide, cut out the appliqués and sew them to the coaster top. Machine quilt all the layers, making rows $\frac{1}{4}$" apart. Place another layer of batting under the quilted coaster top. Attach the coaster bottom, following the directions for the place mat below. *See Figure 1.*

2. To make the place mat, lay the place mat top, right side up, on the quilt batting. Sew the oak leaf appliqué in place, following the instructions in the sidebar on page 88. Machine quilt all the layers together, making rows $\frac{3}{8}$" apart and covering the entire mat. Lay the place mat top on the place mat bottom, right sides together. Stitch around all four sides, rounding the corners and leaving a gap approximately 6" long on one side. Turn the place mat right side out. Fold the edges of the gap toward the wrong side and stitch closed. Topstitch around the edge of the place mat. *See Figure 2.*

3. To make the tray, lay the tray top, right side up, on the quilt batting. Using the template on page 89 as a guide, cut out the oak leaf appliqué and attach it to the tray top following the instructions in the

sidebar below. Machine quilt all the layers together, making rows ⅜" apart and covering the entire tray. Place another layer of batting under the quilted tray top. Mark the finished shape of the tray top on the fabric and cut around it, leaving a seam allowance.

Attach a piece of fusible interfacing to the wrong side of the tray bottom, following the manufacturer's instructions. Mark the finished shape of the tray bottom on the fabric and cut around it, leaving a seam allowance. Place the tray top on the tray bottom, rights sides together, and stitch around all sides, leaving a gap on one side approximately 6". Cut slits in the corners of the tray to allow the sides to fold up. Turn the tray right side out. Fold the edges of the gap toward the wrong side and stitch closed. Topstitch around the tray. Fold the sides up and hand stitch the corners together. Sew the pompoms on top of all four corners. *See Figure 3.*

HOW TO APPLIQUÉ THE OAK LEAF

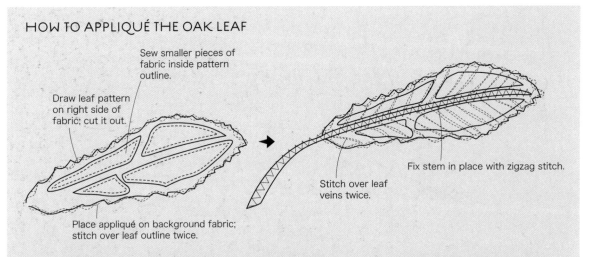

Sew smaller pieces of fabric inside pattern outline.

Draw leaf pattern on right side of fabric; cut it out.

Fix stem in place with zigzag stitch.

Stitch over leaf veins twice.

Place appliqué on background fabric; stitch over leaf outline twice.

Using the template as a guide, draw the leaves on the right side of the fabric; cut out the shape. Cut out smaller pieces of appliqué fabric and place them randomly within the leaf outlines. Place the appliqués on your background fabric. Using the free motion setting on your sewing machine, stitch over the outline and then the veins of the leaves twice with black thread. Use a zigzag stitch to secure the stems.

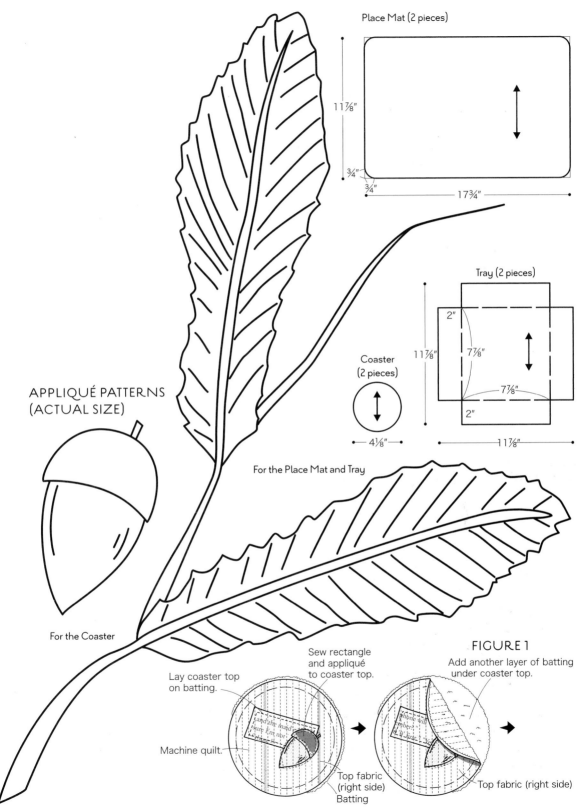

APPLIQUÉ PATTERNS
(ACTUAL SIZE)

For the Coaster

Place Mat (2 pieces)

11⅞"

¾"

¾"

17¾"

Tray (2 pieces)

2"

7⅞"

11⅞"

7⅞"

2"

11⅞"

Coaster
(2 pieces)

4⅛"

For the Place Mat and Tray

Lay coaster top
on batting.

Sew rectangle
and appliqué
to coaster top.

Machine quilt.

Top fabric
(right side)
Batting

FIGURE 1

Add another layer of batting
under coaster top.

Top fabric (right side)

89

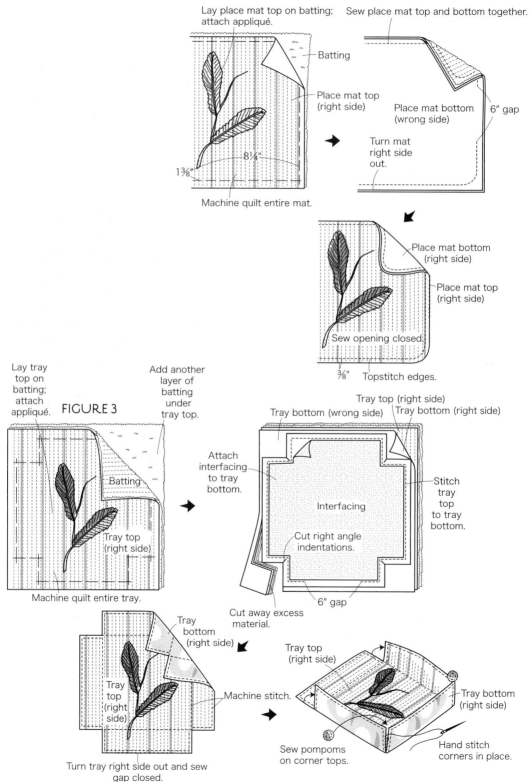

FIGURE 2

Lay place mat top on batting; attach appliqué.

Sew place mat top and bottom together.

Batting

Place mat top (right side)

Place mat bottom (wrong side)

6" gap

Turn mat right side out.

8¼"

1⅜"

Machine quilt entire mat.

Place mat bottom (right side)

Place mat top (right side)

Sew opening closed.

⅜"

Topstitch edges.

FIGURE 3

Lay tray top on batting; attach appliqué.

Add another layer of batting under tray top.

Batting

Tray top (right side)

Machine quilt entire tray.

Tray bottom (wrong side)

Tray top (right side)

Tray bottom (right side)

Attach interfacing to tray bottom.

Interfacing

Stitch tray top to tray bottom.

Cut right angle indentations.

6" gap

Cut away excess material.

Tray bottom (right side)

Tray top (right side)

Machine stitch.

Turn tray right side out and sew gap closed.

Tray top (right side)

Tray bottom (right side)

Sew pompoms on corner tops.

Hand stitch corners in place.

MINIBAG

Photograph on page 27

MATERIALS

- Fabric scraps for patchwork (14 different prints; the patterns are up to you)
- Fabric for gussets and binding (checks): 7⅞" × 19¾" *or* replace binding with bias tape (double fold): ¼" × 19¾"
- Lining (print): 19¾" × 7⅞"
- Leather straps *or* ready-made leather handles (2): ⅛" wide × 14¾" long

FINISHED MEASUREMENTS

The measurements shown for the patchwork pieces include a ¼" seam allowance. The measurements for the lining and gussets are finished measurements; add seam allowances before cutting your fabric. *See Figure 1.*

INSTRUCTIONS

1. Create the patchwork; for block A, sew seven of the fabric strips together in rows. Press the seams open and cut the block horizontally into 1½" strips. Repeat for block B. Sew the patchwork strips together vertically, alternating strips from blocks A and B.

   Stitch the patchwork panels and the gusset fabric together to make the bag exterior. Lay the bag exterior, right side up, on the batting and sew the two layers together using zigzag stitches along the patchwork seams. Machine quilt the gusset fabric, making rows ⅜" apart. *See Figure 2.*

2. Fold the bag exterior in half right sides together; align the edge of the patchwork with the gusset fabric and sew to form a cylinder. Fold the lining fabric in half; align the edges and sew to form a cylinder. Place the lining inside the bag exterior, wrong sides together.

   Take a piece of fabric for the binding 1" wide. Fold the long edges to the center and press. Open up one side and align the raw edge with the right side of the bag top; sew in the fold around the bag top. Fold the binding over the bag top and hand stitch in place to the lining.

   Form the gusset by pressing the bag flat while folding the sides in toward the bag center until just ¾" of the gusset fabric is visible on each side of the patchwork on the front and back. Insert the ends of the handles inside the corner folds of the gussets and sew in place. Each handle should be 14¾" long, with a finished measurement of 12¾".

   Stitch the binding to the bottom edge of the bag front; fold it over to the bag back and hand stitch the binding in place. *See Figure 3.*

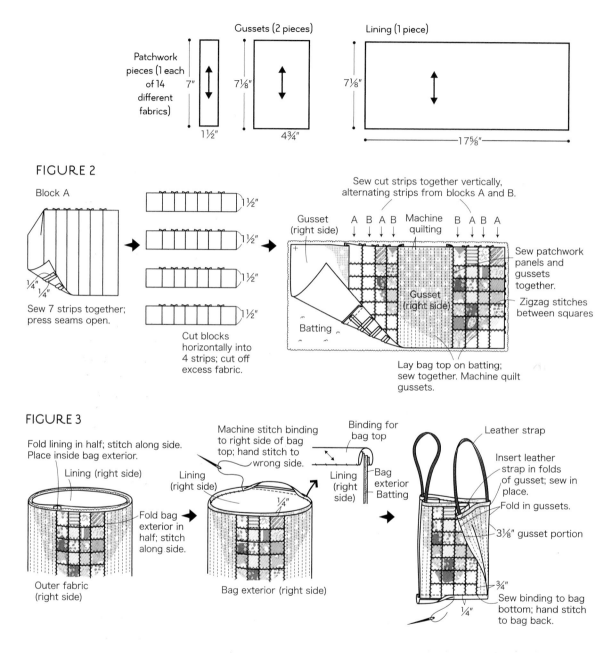

FIGURE 1

Patchwork pieces (1 each of 14 different fabrics)

7"

1½"

Gussets (2 pieces)

7⅛"

4¾"

Lining (1 piece)

7⅛"

17⅝"

FIGURE 2

Block A

Sew 7 strips together; press seams open.

¼" ¼"

1½"
1½"
1½"
1½"

Cut blocks horizontally into 4 strips; cut off excess fabric.

Sew cut strips together vertically, alternating strips from blocks A and B.

Gusset (right side)

A B A B Machine quilting B A B A

Gusset (right side)

Batting

Sew patchwork panels and gussets together.

Zigzag stitches between squares

Lay bag top on batting; sew together. Machine quilt gussets.

FIGURE 3

Fold lining in half; stitch along side. Place inside bag exterior.

Lining (right side)

Fold bag exterior in half; stitch along side.

Outer fabric (right side)

Machine stitch binding to right side of bag top; hand stitch to wrong side.

Lining (right side)

Binding for bag top

Lining (right side)

Bag exterior

Batting

¼"

Bag exterior (right side)

Leather strap

Insert leather strap in folds of gusset; sew in place.

Fold in gussets.

3⅛" gusset portion

¾"

¼"

Sew binding to bag bottom; hand stitch to bag back.

TOTE BAG

Photograph on page 28–29

MATERIALS

- Fabric scraps for patchwork (5 different prints): $3\frac{1}{2}$" × $11\frac{7}{8}$"
- Fabric scraps for patchwork (horizontal stripes): $3\frac{1}{2}$" × $11\frac{7}{8}$"
- Fabric scraps for patchwork (vertical stripes): $3\frac{1}{2}$" × $11\frac{7}{8}$"
- Fabric for contrasting rows, bottom, and lining (cotton, solid color): $35\frac{1}{2}$" × $27\frac{1}{2}$"
- Quilt batting: $27\frac{1}{2}$" × $15\frac{3}{4}$"
- Ready-made leather handles with metal clips (2): $16\frac{1}{2}$" long

FINISHED MEASUREMENTS

All measurements for the patchwork fabric, contrasting fabric, and bag bottom include a $\frac{1}{4}$" seam allowance. *See Figure 1.*

INSTRUCTIONS

1. Create the patchwork; for block A, sew four of the fabric strips together in rows to make a square. Press the seams open and cut the block horizontally into $3\frac{1}{2}$" wide strips. Repeat for block B. Sew the cut strips together horizontally, alternating strips from blocks A and B and the contrasting fabric as shown.

    Place the bag front, right side up, on the batting, and sew the layers together using zigzag stitches along all seams. Machine quilt the contrasting fabric, making rows $\frac{1}{4}$" apart. Repeat for the bag back. *See Figure 2.*

2. Lay the bag front on the bag back, right sides together, and stitch around the bottom and both sides. Turn the bag right side out. Form gussets by flattening the bottom corners of the bag to a width of $3\frac{3}{4}$" or so that the bag bottom ends at the patchwork seams. Stitch in place and leave the corners. *See Figure 3.*

3. Make the interior pocket following the instructions on page 71 and attach it to the lining back. Place the lining front on the lining back, right sides together, and stitch along the bottom and both sides, leaving a gap approximately $4\frac{3}{4}$" long in the bottom seam. Form gussets by flattening the bottom corners to a width of $3\frac{3}{4}$" and stitch across. Cut away the excess fabric. *See Figure 4.*

4. Place the bag exterior inside the lining, right sides together, and stitch around the bag top. Turn the bag right side out using the gap in the lining. *See Figure 5.*

5. Sew the gap in the lining closed. Topstitch around the bag top. Attach the handles to the bag top. *See Figure 6.*

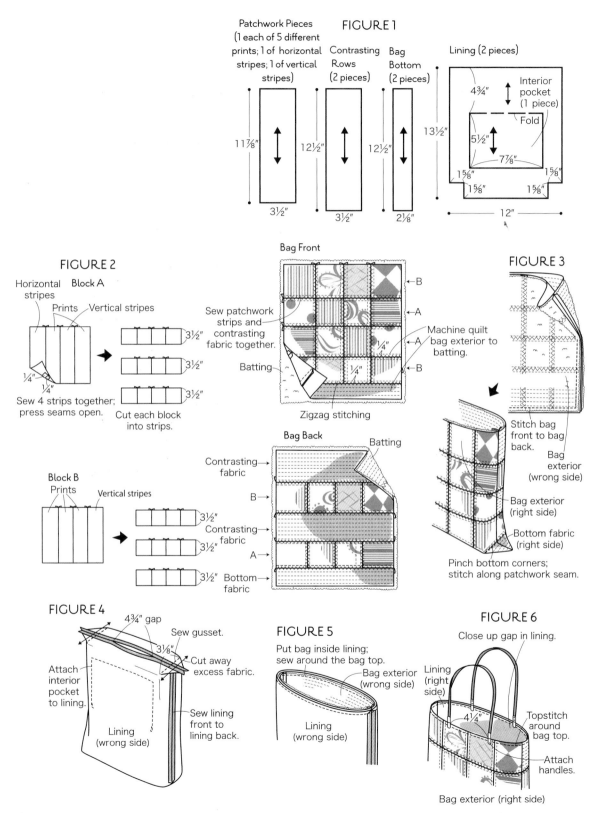

Patchwork Pieces
(1 each of 5 different prints; 1 of horizontal stripes; 1 of vertical stripes)

FIGURE 1

Contrasting Rows (2 pieces)

Bag Bottom (2 pieces)

Lining (2 pieces)

Interior pocket (1 piece)

Fold

11⅞"   12½"   12½"   13½"

4¾"   5½"   7⅞"

3½"   3½"   2⅛"

1⅝"   1⅝"   1⅝"   1⅝"

12"

FIGURE 2

Block A

Horizontal stripes
Prints   Vertical stripes

¼"
¼"

Sew 4 strips together; press seams open.

Cut each block into strips.

3½"
3½"
3½"

Block B
Prints   Vertical stripes

3½"
3½"
3½"

Bag Front

Sew patchwork strips and contrasting fabric together.

Batting

Zigzag stitching

B
A
A
B

¼"
¼"

Machine quilt bag exterior to batting.

Bag Back

Batting

Contrasting fabric

B

Contrasting fabric

A

Bottom fabric

FIGURE 3

Stitch bag front to bag back.

Bag exterior (wrong side)

Bag exterior (right side)

Bottom fabric (right side)

Pinch bottom corners; stitch along patchwork seam.

FIGURE 4

4¾" gap

Sew gusset.

3⅛"

Cut away excess fabric.

Attach interior pocket to lining.

Sew lining front to lining back.

Lining (wrong side)

FIGURE 5

Put bag inside lining; sew around the bag top.

Bag exterior (wrong side)

Lining (wrong side)

FIGURE 6

Close up gap in lining.

Lining (right side)

4¼"

Topstitch around bag top.

Attach handles.

Bag exterior (right side)

LAP QUILT

Photograph on page 30

MATERIALS

- Fabric scraps for patchwork (20 different patterns, including prints, checks, and stripes): 3½" × 19¾" each
- Fabric for blanket back (wool): 55⅜" × 43¼"
- Rickrack: ½" wide × 20 yards long

FINISHED MEASUREMENTS

Add all seam allowances before cutting your fabric. *See Figure 1.*

INSTRUCTIONS

1. Cut strips of fabric 3½" × 19¾" for the patchwork. Create the patchwork by sewing the fabric strips together in rows, using a seam allowance of ⅜". Press the seams open and trim the patchwork block so that it measures 18½" × 17½". Cut the pieced fabric horizontally into 3½" wide strips. Repeat the process to create four different blocks, and cut them into strips. Arrange the strips randomly so that no one pattern or color appears in adjoining squares; sew the strips together. *See Figure 2.*

2. Center the blanket top on the blanket back, wrong sides together. Baste the layers together just inside the edge of the patchwork. Lay rickrack on the horizontal and vertical seams of the patchwork, and sew them in place with a zigzag stitch. Cut away the excess fabric at the corners. Create the blanket border by folding the outside edge of the blanket back ⅜" toward the wrong side. Fold the outside edge again 3½" to cover the raw edges of the patchwork. Hand stitch the blanket back to the patchwork; hand stitch the corners together. Sew the rickrack in place along the inside edge of border with a zigzag stitch. *See Figure 3.*

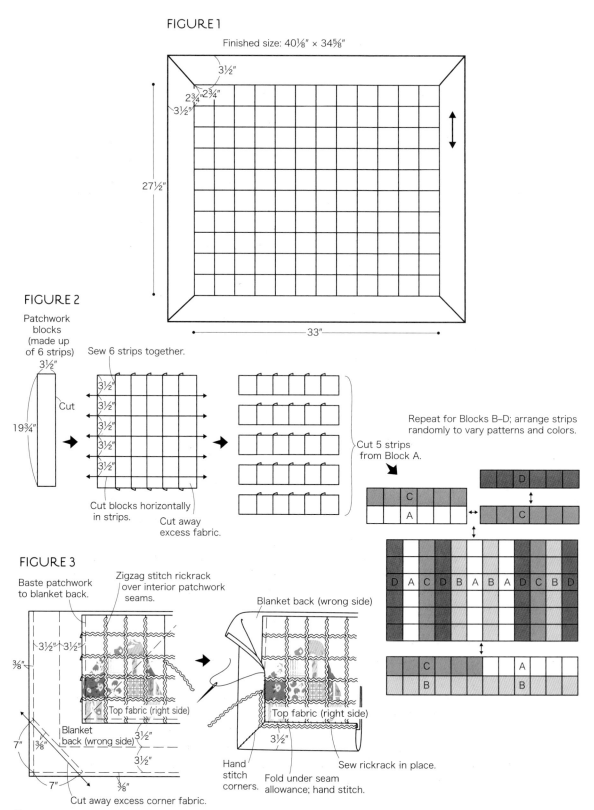

FIGURE 1

Finished size: 40⅛" × 34⅝"

3½"

2¾" 2¾"

3½"

27½"

33"

FIGURE 2

Patchwork blocks (made up of 6 strips)

3½"

Cut

19¾"

Sew 6 strips together.

3½"
3½"
3½"
3½"
3½"

Cut blocks horizontally in strips.

Cut away excess fabric.

Cut 5 strips from Block A.

Repeat for Blocks B–D; arrange strips randomly to vary patterns and colors.

D

C
A

C

D A C D B A B A D C B D

C   A
B   B

FIGURE 3

Baste patchwork to blanket back.

Zigzag stitch rickrack over interior patchwork seams.

Blanket back (wrong side)

3½" 3½"

⅜"

Top fabric (right side)

Blanket back (wrong side)

3½"
3½"

7"

⅜"

7"

⅜"

Cut away excess corner fabric.

Top fabric (right side)

3½"

Hand stitch corners.

Fold under seam allowance; hand stitch.

Sew rickrack in place.

96

FAN-SHAPED BAG

Photograph on page 32

MATERIALS

- Fabric scraps for patchwork (8 different patterns, including prints, stripes, and checks): 7⅞" × 11⅞" each
- Lining (grosgrain): 35½" × 19¾"
- Batting: 35½" × 21⅝"
- Ribbon: ⅝" wide × 4" long
- Leather straps *or* ready-made handles (2): ¼" wide × 21½" long
- Magnetic button (1): ¾" in diameter
- Fusible interfacing for magnetic button

FINISHED MEASUREMENTS

Add all seam allowances before cutting your fabric. *See Figure 1.*

INSTRUCTIONS

1. Mark the finished outline of the bag on the batting and use this as a guide for arranging the patchwork strips. Place the first strip right side up on the batting, making sure the edges of the fabric extend past the outline enough to create a seam allowance. Machine quilt the strip in place, making rows ¼" apart and parallel to the long edge of the strip. Lay the second patchwork strip on top of the first one, right sides together. Stitch it in place, fold it back, and machine quilt it as you did the first one. Continue in this manner until the entire outline has been filled. Repeat for the bag back. *See Figure 2.*

2. Mark the finished shape of the bag on the fabric for the bag front and back and baste ¼" outside the marked lines; cut around the outline, leaving a seam allowance. Lay the bag front on the bag back, right sides together, and stitch around the sides and bottom, starting and stopping 3⅛" from the bag top.

   Prepare two leather straps, each 21 ½" long, and machine baste the ends to the right sides of the bag front and bag back, close to the sides of the bag. The leather straps should extend past the edge of the bag top. (The finished length of the handle is 20".) Fold the decorative ribbon tab and baste it to the right side of the bag front as shown. Turn the bag right side out. *See Figure 3.*

3. Hem the top of the interior pocket by folding the top edge of the fabric twice toward the wrong side and stitching it in place. Lay the pocket, wrong side down, on the right side of the lining back and stitch along the sides and bottom, close to the edge. Stitch down the center of the pocket fabric to create two pouches. Place the lining front on the lining back, right sides together, and stitch along the bottom and both sides, leaving a gap 6" long in the bottom and starting and stopping 3⅛" from the bag top. *See Figure 4.*

4. Place the bag lining over the bag exterior, right sides together. Stitch around the bag top and along the sides of the bag opening. Turn the bag right side out through the opening in the lining; stitch the opening closed. Attach the magnetic button following the instructions on page 101. *See Figure 5.*

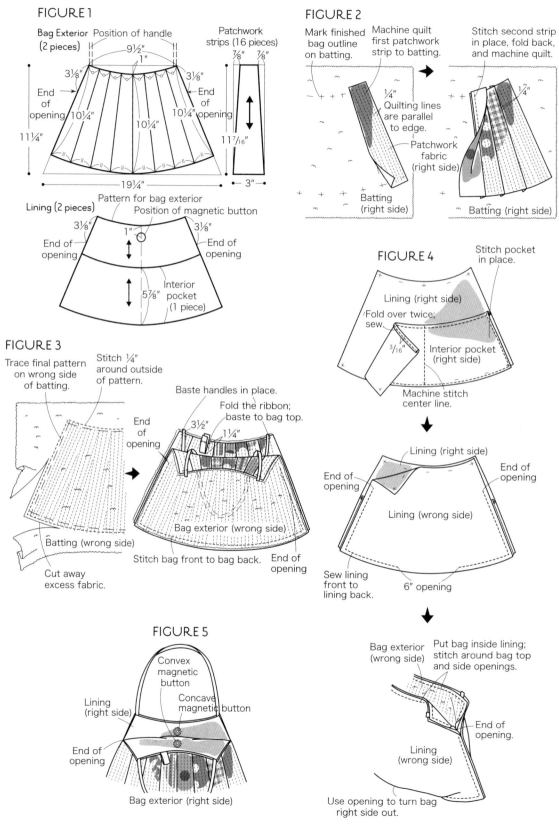

FIGURE 1

Bag Exterior (2 pieces)   Position of handle
9½"
1"
3⅛"   3⅛"
End of opening   10¼"   End of opening   10¼"
11¼"
10¼"
19¼"

Patchwork strips (16 pieces)
⅞"   ⅞"
11⁷⁄₁₆"
3"

Lining (2 pieces)
Pattern for bag exterior
Position of magnetic button
3⅛"   3⅛"
1"
End of opening   End of opening
5⅞"   Interior pocket (1 piece)

FIGURE 2

Mark finished bag outline on batting.   Machine quilt first patchwork strip to batting.   Stitch second strip in place, fold back, and machine quilt.

¼"
Quilting lines are parallel to edge.
Patchwork fabric (right side)
Batting (right side)

¼"
Batting (right side)

FIGURE 4

Stitch pocket in place.
Lining (right side)
Fold over twice; sew.
3⁄16"
Interior pocket (right side)
Machine stitch center line.

Lining (right side)
End of opening   End of opening
Lining (wrong side)
Sew lining front to lining back.
6" opening

FIGURE 3

Trace final pattern on wrong side of batting.   Stitch ¼" around outside of pattern.

Baste handles in place.
Fold the ribbon; baste to bag top.
End of opening   3½"   1¼"

Batting (wrong side)
Cut away excess fabric.

Bag exterior (wrong side)
Stitch bag front to bag back.   End of opening

Bag exterior (wrong side)
Put bag inside lining; stitch around bag top and side openings.

End of opening.
Lining (wrong side)
Use opening to turn bag right side out.

FIGURE 5

Convex magnetic button
Concave magnetic button
Lining (right side)
End of opening
Bag exterior (right side)

POCKET TISSUE CASE

Photograph on page 33

MATERIALS

- Lace and ribbon (4 different kinds total): $9\frac{7}{8}$" each
- Tiny round beads of your choice
- Fabric for bag exterior (chintz, polka dots): $7\frac{7}{8}$" × $9\frac{7}{8}$"
- Fabric for lining and backing (chintz, solid color): $13\frac{3}{4}$" × $11\frac{7}{8}$"
- Quilt batting: $7\frac{7}{8}$" × $9\frac{7}{8}$"
- Sew-on snap (1)

FINISHED MEASUREMENTS

Add all seam allowances before cutting your fabric. *See Figure 1.*

INSTRUCTIONS

1. Lay the case front fabric, right side up, on the batting and backing. Arrange the ribbons and lace in a pattern you like and stitch them to the case front. Attach small beads to the ribbons and lace as you like. *See Figure 2.*

2. Lay piece A on piece B, right sides together, aligning the edges along three sides. Starting ¼" from the top edge, stitch for ⅞" in from each side as shown. Lay piece C on piece B and repeat. Press the seams open. Fold each side of the seam allowance under toward the wrong side and stitch in place. *See Figure 3.*

3. Lay the lining on the case front, right sides together, and stitch all the way around. Turn the pouch right side out through one of the tissue openings. *See Figure 4.*

4. Prick stitch (or backstitch) around the outside edges of the case. Machine stitch across the center of the case to create the fold line. Sew the snap to the case as shown. *See Figure 5.*

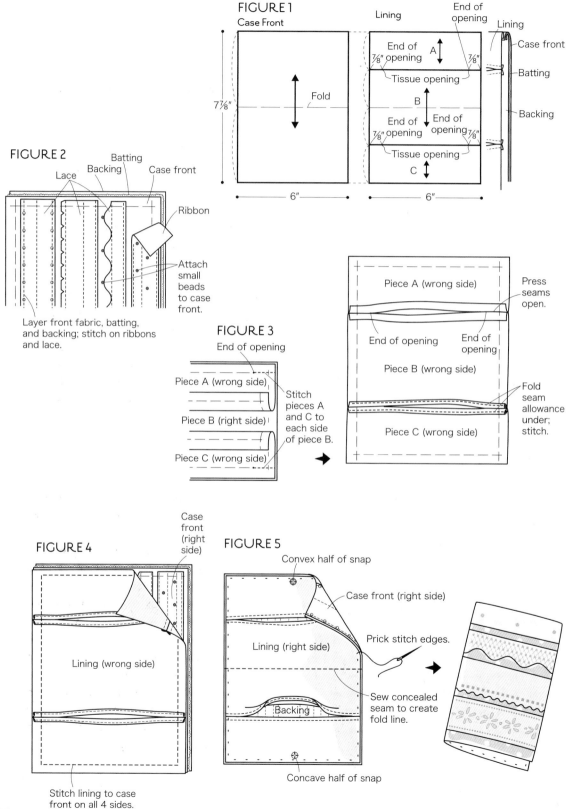

FIGURE 1

Case Front

Lining

End of opening

Lining

Case front

End of opening
7⅞" opening   7⅞"
A
Tissue opening

Batting

7⅞"

Fold

B

Backing

End of opening   End of opening
7⅞" opening   7⅞"
Tissue opening

C

6"   6"

FIGURE 2

Lace   Batting   Backing   Case front

Ribbon

Attach small beads to case front.

Layer front fabric, batting, and backing; stitch on ribbons and lace.

FIGURE 3

End of opening

Piece A (wrong side)

Piece B (right side)

Piece C (wrong side)

Stitch pieces A and C to each side of piece B.

Piece A (wrong side)

Press seams open.

End of opening   End of opening

Piece B (wrong side)

Fold seam allowance under; stitch.

Piece C (wrong side)

FIGURE 4

Case front (right side)

Lining (wrong side)

Stitch lining to case front on all 4 sides.

FIGURE 5

Convex half of snap

Case front (right side)

Prick stitch edges.

Lining (right side)

Sew concealed seam to create fold line.

Backing

Concave half of snap

100

FAN-SHAPED MINIBAG

Photograph on page 35

MATERIALS

- Fabric scraps for patchwork (12 different prints; the colors and patterns are up to you)
- Lining (cotton, solid color): 31½" × 7⅞"
- Quilt batting: 23⅝" × 7⅞"
- Leather strap: ³/₁₆" wide × 12" long
- Magnetic button (1): ½" in diameter
- Fusible interfacing for magnetic button

FINISHED MEASUREMENTS

All measurements for the patchwork fabric include a ¼" seam allowance. All measurements for the bag exterior, lining, and pocket are finished measurements; add seam allowances before cutting your fabric. *See Figure 1.*

INSTRUCTIONS

1. Sew the fan patchwork for the bag front and back, following the instructions on page 97.

   Adhere a piece of fusible interfacing to the wrong side of the fabric for the front top band, following the manufacturer's instructions. Fold the seam allowance of the bottom edge under. Position the top band on the batting, right side up, with the bottom edge over the seam allowance of top of the bag front; stitch in place. Machine quilt the top band, making the rows ¼" apart and parallel to the top edge. *See Figure 2.*

HOW TO ATTACH THE MAGNETIC BUTTON

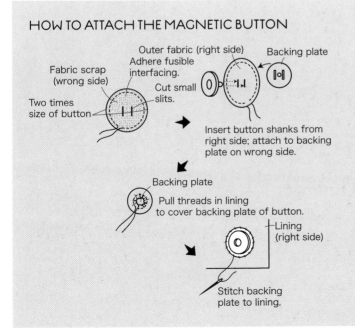

Fabric scrap (wrong side)

Two times size of button

Outer fabric (right side)
Adhere fusible interfacing.
Cut small slits.

Backing plate

Insert button shanks from right side; attach to backing plate on wrong side.

Backing plate

Pull threads in lining to cover backing plate of button.

Lining (right side)

Stitch backing plate to lining.

Attach a piece of fusible interfacing to the wrong side of a piece of fabric twice the size of your button. Using small stitches, sew around the edge of the fabric, leaving two tails of thread. Cut two small slits in the center of the fabric to accommodate the shanks of the button. Push the shanks through the right side of the fabric and secure them in place with the backing plate. Pull the loose threads tight, covering the backing plate of the button with the fabric. Hand stitch the backing plate to the lining.

2. Follow the instructions on page 97 to make the lining and the interior pocket.

3. Place the bag front on the bag back, right sides together, and stitch along the sides and bottom, starting and stopping 1 ½" from the bag top. Baste one end of the leather strap to the right side of the bag front and the other end to the back as shown. (The finished measurement of the handle is 11".) Place the bag lining over the bag exterior, right sides together, and sew along the bag top. Turn the bag right side out. *See Figure 3.*

4. Following the instructions on page 101, attach the magnetic button to the lining.

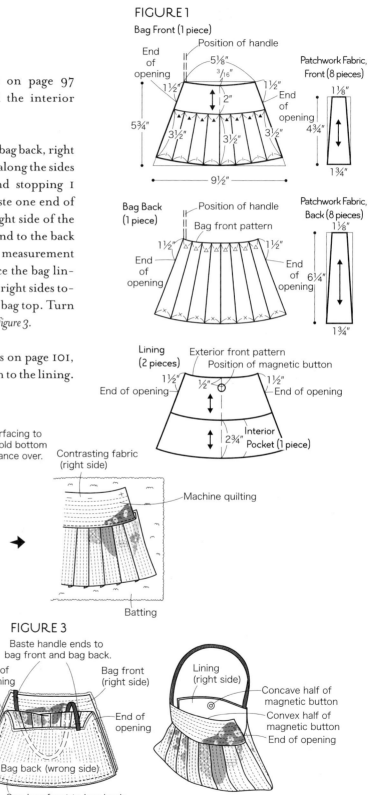

FIGURE 1
Bag Front (1 piece)
Position of handle
End of opening
5⅛"
³/₁₆"
1½"
2"
End of opening
1½"
5¾"
3½" 3½" 3½"
9½"

Patchwork Fabric, Front (8 pieces)
1⅛"
4¾"
1¾"

Bag Back (1 piece)
Position of handle
Bag front pattern
1½"
End of opening
1½"
End of opening

Patchwork Fabric, Back (8 pieces)
1⅛"
6¼"
1¾"

Lining (2 pieces)
Exterior front pattern
Position of magnetic button
1½" ½"
End of opening
1½"
End of opening
Interior Pocket (1 piece)
2¾"

FIGURE 2
Top band
Fusible interfacing
Attach interfacing to top band; fold bottom seam allowance over.
Top band (right side)
Stitch in place.
Batting
Sew patchwork fabric to batting.

Contrasting fabric (right side)
Machine quilting
Batting

FIGURE 3
Baste handle ends to bag front and bag back.
End of opening
Bag front (right side)
End of opening
Bag back (wrong side)
Sew bag front to bag back.

Lining (right side)
Concave half of magnetic button
Convex half of magnetic button
End of opening

RED AND BLUE PARTY BAGS

Photograph on page 36–37

MATERIALS FOR THE RED BAG (A)

- Fabric scraps for patchwork (kimono cloth, satin, cotton; the colors and patterns are up to you)
- Fabric for ruffles (crepe): $7\frac{7}{8}" \times 11\frac{7}{8}"$
- Fabric for bag back (kimono cloth): $9\frac{7}{8}" \times 5\frac{7}{8}"$
- Fabric for lining and loops (cotton, checks): $15\frac{3}{4}" \times 11\frac{7}{8}"$
- Quilt batting: $23\frac{5}{8}" \times 5\frac{7}{8}"$
- Fusible interfacing for lining: $15\frac{3}{4}" \times 11\frac{7}{8}"$
- Cord for strap: $\frac{1}{8}"$ wide $\times 39\frac{3}{8}"$ long
- Magnetic button (1): $\frac{1}{2}"$ in diameter

MATERIALS FOR THE BLUE BAG (B)

- Fabric scraps for patchwork (prints, satin, solid color; the colors and patterns are up to you)
- Fabric for bag back (print): $9\frac{7}{8}" \times 5\frac{7}{8}"$
- Fabric for lining and loops (solid color cotton): $15\frac{3}{8}" \times 11\frac{7}{8}"$
- Quilt batting: $23\frac{5}{8}" \times 15\frac{7}{8}"$
- Adhesive backing for lining: $15\frac{3}{4}" \times 11\frac{7}{8}"$
- Decorative tape for edges: $\frac{1}{4}"$ wide $\times 19\frac{3}{4}"$ long
- Strap for loop: $3\frac{1}{8}"$
- Magnetic button (1): $\frac{1}{8}"$

FINISHED MEASUREMENTS

Add all seam allowances before cutting your fabric. *See Figure 1.*

INSTRUCTIONS

1. Mark the finished outline of the bag front (see page 106) on the batting and use this as a guide for arranging the patchwork strips. Place the first strip right side up on the batting, making sure the edges of the fabric extend past the outline enough to create a seam allowance; sew in place. Lay the second patchwork strip on top of the first one, right sides together. Stitch it in place and open up the fabric. Continue in this manner until the entire outline has been filled. Zigzag stitch along all the seams and machine quilt all or some of the fabric strips, making rows $\frac{3}{16}"$ apart. *See Figure 2.*

2. For bag A, cut the crepe fabric for the ruffles at $\frac{5}{8}"$ intervals along the short side, then tear strips off by hand. Hand stitch a straight line down the center of each fabric strip. Pull the tails of the thread to reduce the $11\frac{7}{8}"$ length to $5\frac{7}{8}"$. Sew the gathered ruffles in place on the bag front. Cut around the bag outline, leaving a seam allowance.

   Pinch the fabric for the darts on the wrong side; align and then sew along the marked lines. Press the seam allowance toward the center. *See Figure 3.*

3. For bag B, pinch the fabric for the darts on the wrong side; align and then sew along the marked lines. Press the seam allowance toward the center. Position the decorative tape along the edge of the bag, just inside the seam allowance, and baste in place. *See Figure 4.*

4. Lay the fabric for the bag back, right side up, on the batting. Pinch the fabric for

the darts on the wrong side, aligning and then sewing along the marked lines. Press the seam allowance toward the center. Place the bag front on the bag back, right sides together, and stitch along the sides and bottom. Turn the bag right side out.

For bag A, make two tabs, using two pieces of fabric 1" × 1¼". Fold the long edges toward the center and then fold it in half again lengthwise. Machine stitch along the long edge.

For bag B, make two loops out of cord, both 1¼" long.

Baste each tab/loop to the right side of each side seam near the bag top; the finished height of each will be ¼". See Figure 5.

5. Adhere fusible interfacing to the wrong side of the lining fabric according to the manufacturer's instructions. Make the interior pocket following the instructions on page 71 and attach it to the lining back. Sew the darts in the lining front and lining back. Place the lining front on the lining back, right sides together, and stitch along the bottom and both sides, leaving a gap approximately 4" long in the bottom seam. Place the bag lining over the bag exterior, right sides together, and stitch along the bag top. Turn the bag right side out through the gap in the lining. Sew the gap closed. See Figure 6.

6. Pass the ends of the strap through the fabric loops at the top of the bag. (For bag A, the finished length of the strap is 37⅜"; for bag B, it is 15¾".) Use fabric glue to fix the ends of the strap in place, then wrap thread around them. Attach the magnetic button, following the instructions on page 101. Prick stitch (or backstitch) along the bag top. See Figure 7.

FIGURE 1

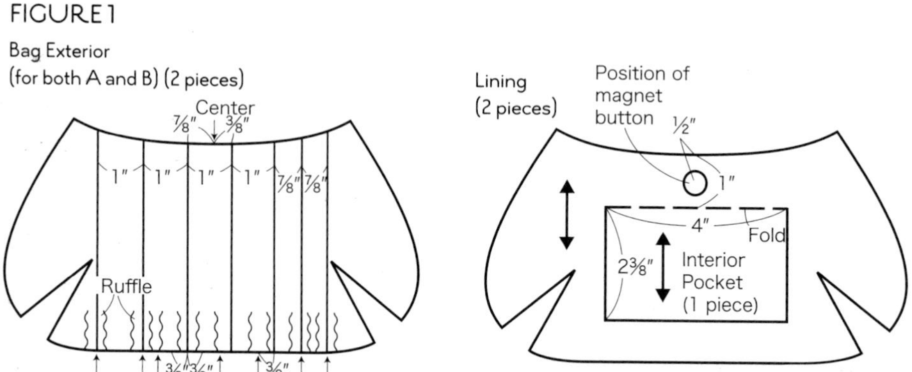

Bag Exterior
(for both A and B) (2 pieces)

Center
⅞" ⅜"
1" 1" 1" 1" ⅞" ⅞"
Ruffle
⅜" ⅜" ¾" ⅜"
Position of ruffles

Lining
(2 pieces)

Position of magnet button ½"

1"
4"
Fold
2⅜"
Interior Pocket
(1 piece)

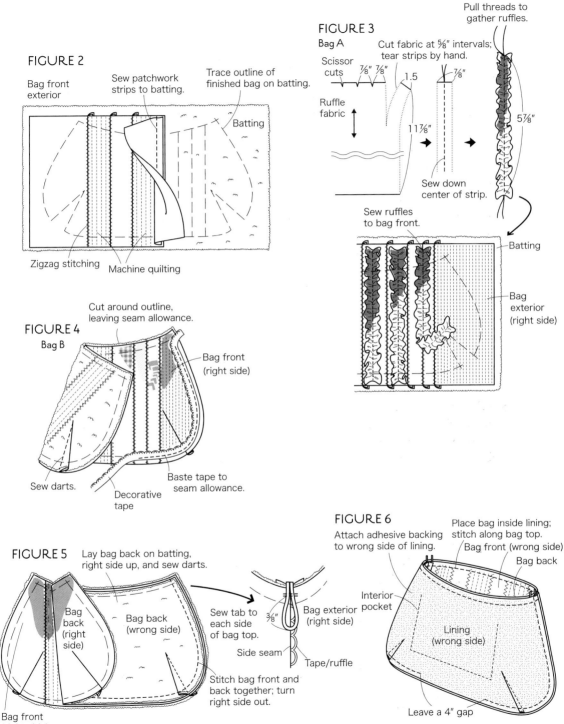

FIGURE 2

Bag front exterior

Sew patchwork strips to batting.

Trace outline of finished bag on batting.

Batting

Zigzag stitching

Machine quilting

FIGURE 3
Bag A

Pull threads to gather ruffles.

Cut fabric at ⅝" intervals; tear strips by hand.

Scissor cuts

⅞" ⅞" 1.5 ⅞"

Ruffle fabric

11⅞"

5⅞"

Sew down center of strip.

Sew ruffles to bag front.

Batting

Bag exterior (right side)

FIGURE 4
Bag B

Cut around outline, leaving seam allowance.

Bag front (right side)

Sew darts.

Decorative tape

Baste tape to seam allowance.

FIGURE 5

Lay bag back on batting, right side up, and sew darts.

Bag back (right side)

Bag back (wrong side)

Bag front (right side)

Sew tab to each side of bag top.

Side seam

⅜"

Bag exterior (right side)

Tape/ruffle

Stitch bag front and back together; turn right side out.

FIGURE 6

Attach adhesive backing to wrong side of lining.

Place bag inside lining; stitch along bag top.

Bag front (wrong side)

Bag back

Interior pocket

Lining (wrong side)

Leave a 4" gap

105

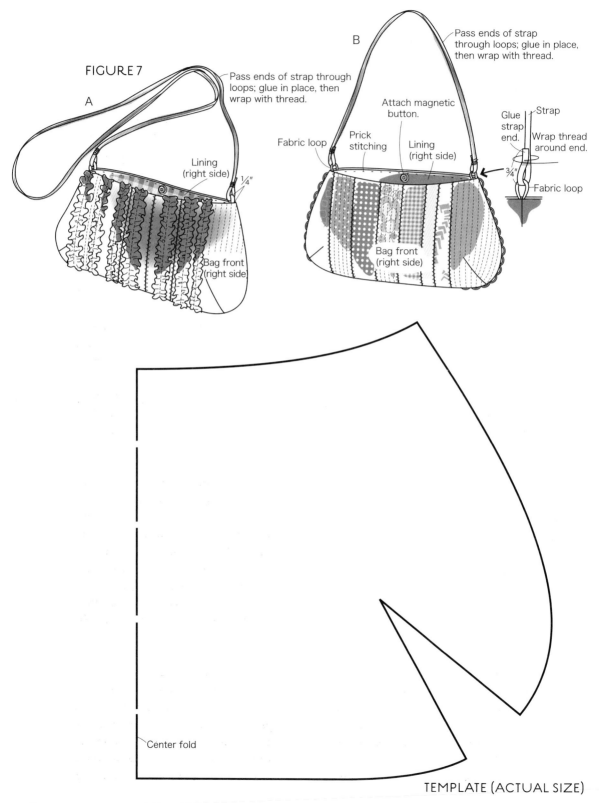

FIGURE 7

A

Pass ends of strap through loops; glue in place, then wrap with thread.

Lining (right side)

¼"

Bag front (right side)

B

Pass ends of strap through loops; glue in place, then wrap with thread.

Attach magnetic button.

Fabric loop

Prick stitching

Lining (right side)

Bag front (right side)

Glue strap end.

Strap

Wrap thread around end.

¾"

Fabric loop

Center fold

TEMPLATE (ACTUAL SIZE)

SHOULDER BAG

Photograph on page 38

MATERIALS

- Fabric scraps for patchwork (prints, solid colors; the patterns and colors are up to you)
- Fabric for bag exterior, handle casing, and lining (cotton chintz, solid colors): $23\frac{5}{8}$" × $19\frac{3}{4}$"
- Fabric for back pocket and pocket lining (print): $15\frac{3}{4}$" × $19\frac{3}{4}$"
- Quilt batting: $25\frac{5}{8}$" × $11\frac{7}{8}$"
- Bias tape for top of front pocket (double fold): $\frac{3}{8}$" wide × $9\frac{7}{8}$" long
- Cord for loops: 4"
- Leather strap: $\frac{3}{8}$" wide × $47\frac{1}{4}$" long
- Swivel snap hooks (2): $\frac{3}{8}$" wide
- Cap rivets (2): $\frac{1}{4}$" in diameter
- Magnetic button (1): $\frac{1}{2}$" in diameter

FINISHED MEASUREMENTS

Add all seam allowances before cutting your fabric. *See Figure 1.*

INSTRUCTIONS

1. Create the front patchwork pocket by sewing two patchwork blocks. For block A, cut 10 fabric strips, 4" × $1\frac{3}{8}$" each. Place the first strip horizontally on the batting; place the second strip on top of it (right sides together); sew through all three layers, leaving a seam allowance of $\frac{3}{8}$" on the fabric strips. Fold the second strip down and attach the third in the same way; keep adding strips until you have a block measuring 4" × $6\frac{5}{8}$".

   For block B, cut 8 strips of fabric, $6\frac{5}{8}$" × 4" each. Sew them to the batting in the same way as for block A, but lay the strips vertically. Keep adding strips until you have a block measuring 7" × $6\frac{5}{8}$". Zigzag stitch over all the seams on blocks A and B. *See Figure 2.*

2. Lay block A on block B, right sides together, and stitch down the left edge to create one piece of fabric. Press the seam open, and zigzag stitch over the seam. Mark the finished shape of the front pocket on the fabric and cut around it, leaving a seam allowance.

   Baste the folded bias tape across the top edge of the pocket. Place the pocket lining on the pocket exterior, right sides together, and sew along the top edge. Fold the lining to the wrong side of the pocket and baste the two layers together along the bottom and both sides. *See Figure 3.*

3. Lay the back pocket fabric right side up on the batting and machine quilt the layers together, making rows $\frac{3}{8}$" apart. Place the back pocket fabric on the back pocket lining, right sides together, and sew along the top edge. Fold the lining over to the wrong side of the pocket and machine stitch the two layers together around the bottom and both sides. *See Figure 4.*

4. Place a piece of batting 9" × $3\frac{1}{2}$" on the wrong side of the top of the exterior bag front; machine quilt the layers together, making rows $\frac{3}{8}$" apart. Place the front pocket, right side up, on the bag front and stitch along the sides and bottom. Sew a concealed seam along

the line between the two patchwork blocks to divide the pocket. Assemble the bag back and pocket in the same way.

Place the handle casing fabric on the batting and fold the layers in half lengthwise with right sides together. Stitch around the three open sides, leaving a 3" gap along the bottom. Turn the handle casing right side out and machine quilt it, making rows ¼" apart and closing the gap. Lay the handle casing on the top of the bag back as shown and sew it in place along the top and bottom. *See Figure 5.*

5. Place the bag front on the bag back, right sides together, and stitch along the bottom and both sides. Take a 2" piece of cord, create a loop, and baste one loop to each side seam on the right side of the bag exterior.

Make the lining following the instructions on page 71. Place the lining front on the lining back, right sides together, and stitch along the bottom and both sides, leaving a gap approximately 4" long in the bottom seam. Place the bag lining over the bag exterior, right sides together, and stitch along the bag top. Turn the bag right side out through the gap in the lining. Stitch around the bag top.

Pass the ends of the leather strap through the swivel snap hooks. Fold the ends against the strap, 1" from the hook. Punch a hole through both layers, and secure in place with a cap rivet. Attach the magnetic button, following the instructions on page 101. *See Figure 6.*

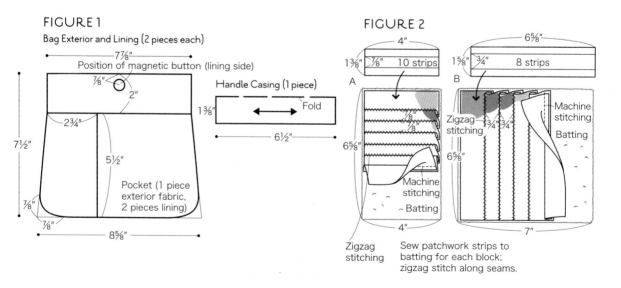

FIGURE 1
Bag Exterior and Lining (2 pieces each)

Handle Casing (1 piece)

Pocket (1 piece exterior fabric, 2 pieces lining)

FIGURE 2

A — 4" — 1⅜" ⅞" 10 strips
B — 6⅝" — 1⅝" ¾" 8 strips

Machine stitching
Zigzag stitching
Batting

Zigzag stitching — Sew patchwork strips to batting for each block; zigzag stitch along seams.

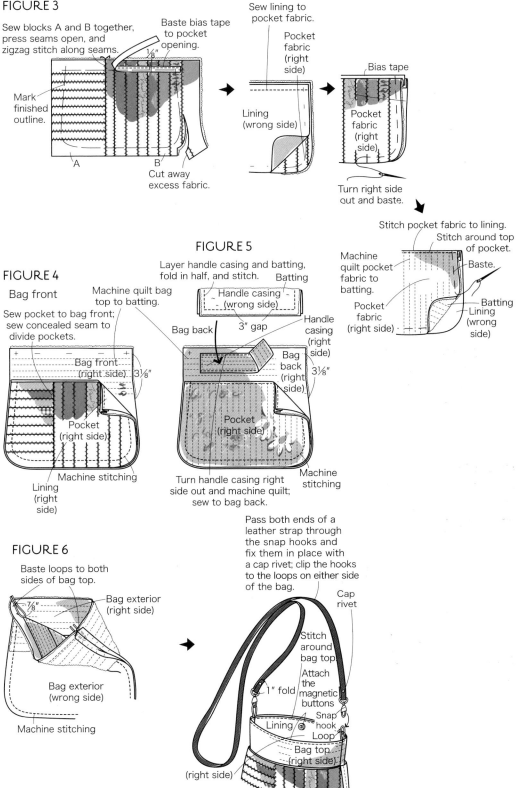

FIGURE 3

Sew blocks A and B together, press seams open, and zigzag stitch along seams.

Baste bias tape to pocket opening.

⅛"

Mark finished outline.

A   B

Cut away excess fabric.

Sew lining to pocket fabric.

Pocket fabric (right side)

Lining (wrong side)

Bias tape

Pocket fabric (right side)

Turn right side out and baste.

Stitch pocket fabric to lining.

Stitch around top of pocket.

Machine quilt pocket fabric to batting.

Pocket fabric (right side)

Baste.

Batting

Lining (wrong side)

FIGURE 4

Bag front

Sew pocket to bag front; sew concealed seam to divide pockets.

Machine quilt bag top to batting.

Bag front (right side)   3⅛"

Pocket (right side)

Machine stitching

Lining (right side)

FIGURE 5

Layer handle casing and batting, fold in half, and stitch.

Batting

Handle casing (wrong side)

3" gap

Bag back

Handle casing (right side)

Bag back (right side)   3⅛"

Pocket (right side)

Turn handle casing right side out and machine quilt; sew to bag back.

Machine stitching

FIGURE 6

Baste loops to both sides of bag top.

⅞"

Bag exterior (right side)

Bag exterior (wrong side)

Machine stitching

Pass both ends of a leather strap through the snap hooks and fix them in place with a cap rivet; clip the hooks to the loops on either side of the bag.

Cap rivet

Stitch around bag top

Attach the magnetic buttons

1" fold

Lining

Snap hook

Loop

Bag top (right side)

(right side)

PILLOW COVER

Photograph on page 40

MATERIALS

- Fabric scraps for patchwork (prints; the patterns and colors are up to you)
- Fabric for center square (grosgrain, solid color): $11\frac{7}{8}$" × $11\frac{7}{8}$"
- Fabric for cushion back (cotton, stripes): $21\frac{5}{8}$" × $19\frac{3}{4}$"
- Backing (cotton print): $19\frac{3}{8}$" × $19\frac{3}{8}$"
- Quilt batting: $19\frac{3}{8}$" × $19\frac{3}{8}$"
- Bias tape: $\frac{3}{4}$" wide × $78\frac{3}{4}$" long
- Zipper (1): $15\frac{3}{4}$" long

FINISHED MEASUREMENTS

Add all seam allowances before cutting your fabric. *See Figure 1.*

INSTRUCTIONS

1. Mark the finished measurements of the pillow on the batting. Place the center square within the outline and machine quilt the square to the batting, making rows $\frac{1}{2}$" apart. Make four patchwork strips measuring $4\frac{1}{2}$" × $19\frac{1}{8}$" each; the finished measurements will be $3\frac{1}{2}$" × $18\frac{1}{8}$". Attach the strips to the cushion top in the order shown, laying each strip on the central square, wrong sides together, and sewing in place with a seam allowance of $\frac{1}{2}$". Machine quilt each strip, making rows $\frac{1}{2}$" apart. *See Figure 2.*

2. Assemble the pillow back according to the instructions on page 69.

3. Baste the pillow top to the backing. Machine stitch around the inside of the square. *See Figure 3.*

4. Place the pillow top on the pillow back, right sides together, and stitch along all four sides. Turn the pillow cover right side out through the open zipper.

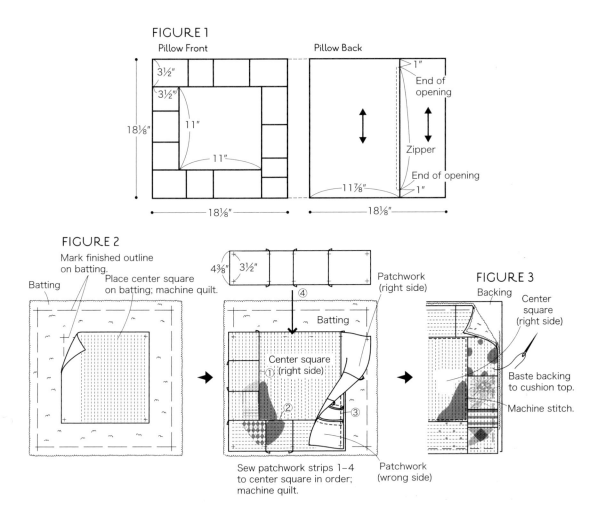

FIGURE 1

Pillow Front

3½"
3½"
18⅛"
11"
11"
18⅛"

Pillow Back

1"
End of opening
Zipper
End of opening
11⅞"
1"
18⅛"

FIGURE 2

Mark finished outline on batting.
Place center square on batting; machine quilt.
Batting

4⅜" 3½"
④

Batting
Patchwork (right side)
Center square ① (right side)
②
③
Patchwork (wrong side)

Sew patchwork strips 1–4 to center square in order; machine quilt.

FIGURE 3

Backing
Center square (right side)
Baste backing to cushion top.
Machine stitch.

III

QUILT

Photograph on page 41

MATERIALS

- Fabric scraps for patchwork (prints; the colors and patterns are up to you)
- Fabric for borders and bindings (cotton, polka dots): 43¼" × 51⅜" *or* (in place of binding) bias tape (double fold): ⅞" × 8 yards
- Fabric for border (corduroy): 11¾" × 39⅜"
- Fabric for back (cotton, print): 43¼" × 149⅝"
- Quilt batting: 35½" × 149⅝"

FINISHED MEASUREMENTS

Add all seam allowances before cutting your fabric. *See Figure 1.*

INSTRUCTIONS

1. Prepare the patchwork fabric for the quilt top by referring to the diagram on page 113 for the widths and cutting to any length you desire. All measurements shown are the finished dimensions, so add a seam allowance to all sides of the pieces before cutting. Using the diagram as a guide, stitch the patchwork pieces together to make vertical strips; press the seams to one side, all in the same direction. Sew all 19 strips together, alternating the direction of the original seam allowances before you sew the strips together; press the seam allowance to one side. *See Figure 2.*

2. Lay the quilt top, right side up, on the batting and back; baste the layers together vertically and diagonally. Divide the quilt top into right and left halves, and machine quilt out from the center, making rows ¾" apart.

    Place the side borders on the patchwork, right sides together, and stitch in place through the four layers. Fold the border out, and machine quilt it, making rows ¾" apart. Repeat for the top and bottom borders. *See Figure 3.*

3. Finish the quilt with bias tape, following the instructions given on page 114.

FIGURE 1

Composite diagram

¼" binding

Finished Quilt—67" × 70⅞"

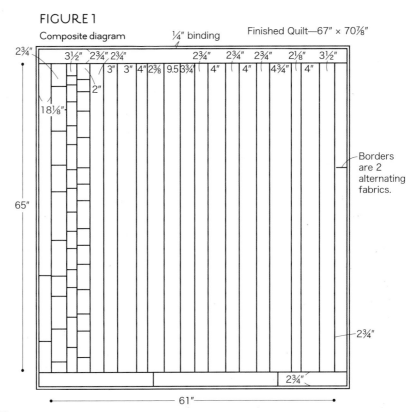

2¾"

3½" 2¾" 2¾" 3" 3" 4" 2⅜ 9.5 3¾ 2¾" 2¾" 2¾" 2⅛" 3½"

3" 3" 4"2⅜ 9.53¾ 4" 4" 4¾" 4"

2"

18⅛"

65"

Borders are 2 alternating fabrics.

2¾"

2¾"

61"

FIGURE 2

Prepare patchwork pieces of various lengths; stitch together to make strips.

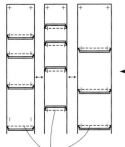

Sew strips together; fold all seam allowances to one side.

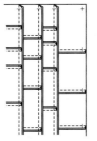

Fold seam allowances on every other strip in same direction.

FIGURE 3

Back (wrong side)

Batting Quilt top (right side)

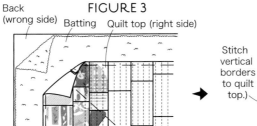

Stitch horizontal borders to quilt top.

Backing

Stitch vertical borders to quilt top.)

Batting

Border (wrong side)

Machine quilt borders.

Machine quilt borders.

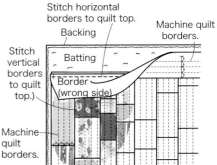

Lay quilt top on batting and backing; baste vertically and diagonally.

Divide quilt top into right and left halves; machine quilt out from center.

HOW TO BIND THE QUILT

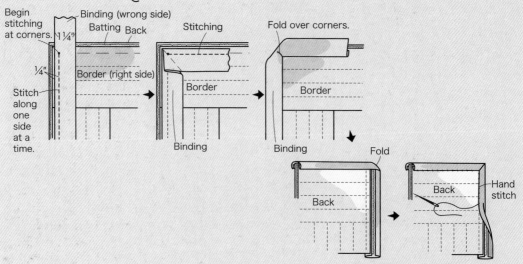

Take a piece of fabric 1¼" wide and press the long edges to the center. Open up the fabric and align the raw edge of the binding with the raw edge of the quilt, right sides together. Starting at one of the corners, stitch the binding in place, ¼" from the edge. When you've finished stitching one side, pinch the corner and fold it toward the finished edge. Continue stitching on the next side. When all sides are done, fold the binding toward the quilt back and hand stitch in place.

POCKET TISSUE CASE

Photograph on page 44

MATERIALS FOR YELLOW TISSUE CASE

- Felt: 6⅜" × 7⅞"
- Buttons (2): ½" × ½"

MATERIALS FOR WHITE TISSUE CASE

- Felt: 13⅜" × 7⅞"
- Ribbon: ⅜" wide × 7⅞" long
- Rickrack: ⅝" wide × 7⅞" long
- Buttons (2): one ½" in diameter; one ¾" in diameter

INSTRUCTIONS

1. For the yellow case, with your sewing machine set for free motion, stitch randomly across the felt with black thread to make a design. Use a rotary cutter with a pinking blade to cut a wavy edge on the short ends of the felt. *See Figure 1.*

2. Fold the short ends of the felt to the center, wrong sides together, leaving a slight opening between them for the tissues. Stitch along both open sides, ⅜" from edge. Backstitch across the center opening, ³⁄₁₆" from the seam on both sides. Use a rotary cutter to cut a wavy edge on both sides. Attach the buttons as shown. *See Figure 2.*

3. For the white case, place the two pieces of felt together; align the ribbon to one of the short sides, and sew through all three layers. Fold the two short sides to the center, with the ribbon on the outside, leaving a slight opening. Trim any excess fabric from the edges of the inside piece to match the outside opening. *See Figure 3.*

4. Unfold the felt and place rickrack along the edge of the opening opposite the ribbon; sew through all three layers. Fold the two short sides to the center again and stitch along both open sides, ⅜" from edge. Backstitch across the center opening, ³⁄₁₆" from the seam on both sides. Use a rotary cutter to cut a wavy edge on both sides. Attach the buttons as shown. *See Figure 4.*

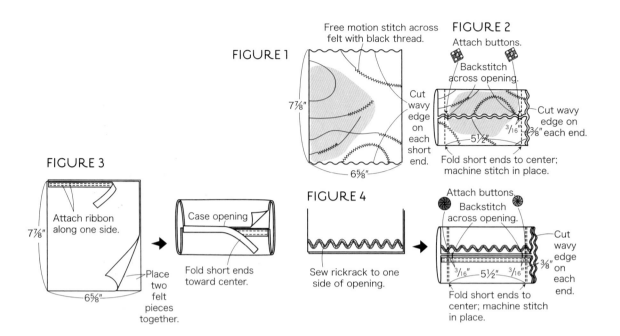

FIGURE 1

Free motion stitch across felt with black thread.

7⅞"

Cut wavy edge on each short end.

6⅝"

FIGURE 2

Attach buttons.

Backstitch across opening.

Cut wavy edge on ⅜" each end.

5½"

³⁄₁₆"

Fold short ends to center; machine stitch in place.

FIGURE 3

Attach ribbon along one side.

7⅞"

6⅝"

Place two felt pieces together.

Case opening

Fold short ends toward center.

FIGURE 4

Sew rickrack to one side of opening.

Attach buttons.

Backstitch across opening.

Cut wavy edge ⅜" on each end.

³⁄₁₆" 5½" ³⁄₁₆"

Fold short ends to center; machine stitch in place.

PILLOW COVER

Photograph on page 46

MATERIALS

- Fabric for patchwork (2 different prints): 13¾" × 4" each
- Fabric for patchwork (solid yellow): 13¾" × 7⅞"
- Fabric for patchwork and back (solid black): 19¾" × 13¾"
- Backing (thin cotton): 13¾" × 13¾"
- Quilt batting: 13¾" × 13¾"
- Bias tape: ¾" wide × 55⅛" long
- Zipper (1): 11" long

FINISHED MEASUREMENTS

Add all seam allowances before cutting your fabric. *See Figure 1.*

INSTRUCTIONS

1. Mark the finished pattern of the pillow on the batting. Position the yellow fabric on the quilt batting and machine quilt, making rows ½" apart. Place the top patterned fabric on the yellow piece, right sides together, and stitch. Fold the top fabric back and machine quilt, making rows ½" apart. Attach the other patterned fabric and black piece in the same way. Using the templates on page 118, trace the Roman numerals on the yellow fabric and machine embroider with your sewing machine. *See Figure 2.*

2. Zigzag stitch over the patchwork seams. Create decorative stitches using the free motion setting on your machine inside the seams on the main panel. Create a design on the bottom panel by machine stitching a combination of zigzag and straight stitches with contrasting thread. Place the pillow top on the backing fabric and baste the layers together around all four sides. *See Figure 3.*

3. Assemble the cushion back, following the instructions on page 69. Place the cushion top on the cushion back, right sides together, and stitch along all four sides. Turn the cushion right side out through the open zipper.

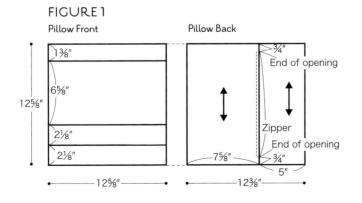

FIGURE 1

Pillow Front

Pillow Back

1⅜"
6⅝"
2⅛"
2⅛"
12⅝"
12⅝"

¾"
End of opening
Zipper
End of opening
7⅝"
¾"
5"
12⅜"

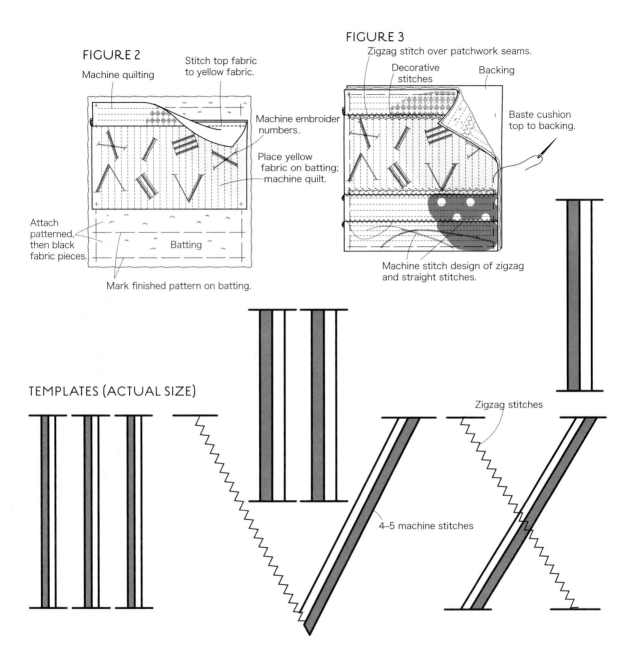

FIGURE 2

Machine quilting

Stitch top fabric to yellow fabric.

Machine embroider numbers.

Place yellow fabric on batting; machine quilt.

Attach patterned, then black fabric pieces.

Batting

Mark finished pattern on batting.

FIGURE 3

Zigzag stitch over patchwork seams.

Decorative stitches

Backing

Baste cushion top to backing.

Machine stitch design of zigzag and straight stitches.

TEMPLATES (ACTUAL SIZE)

Zigzag stitches

4–5 machine stitches

LAP QUILT

Photograph on page 47

MATERIALS

- Fabric for patchwork (solids, prints; the colors and patterns are up to you)
- Fabric for quilt back (wool): $35\frac{3}{8}"$ × $55\frac{1}{8}"$
- Quilt batting: $51\frac{1}{4}"$ × $35\frac{1}{2}"$ long

FINISHED MEASUREMENTS

Add all seam allowances before cutting your fabric. *See Figure 1.*

INSTRUCTIONS

1. Prepare the patchwork fabric for the quilt top by referring to the diagram below for the widths and cutting to any length you desire. All measurements shown are the finished dimensions, so add a seam allowance to all sides of the pieces before cutting. Using the diagram as a guide, stitch the patchwork pieces together to make three rows; press the seams to one side, all in the same direction.

   Mark the finished outline on the batting. Position the middle patchwork row on the batting; machine quilt it in place, making rows $\frac{1}{2}"$ apart on patterned pieces and creating designs with a combination of zigzag and straight stitches on solid pieces. Place the top patchwork row on the middle row, right sides together, and stitch in place; repeat for the bottom row. Fold the top and bottom rows back and machine quilt them in place. Place the right side panel on the quilt top, right sides together, and sew together. Fold the panel back and machine quilt it in place, as with middle row. *See Figure 2.*

2. Place the quilt top on the quilt back, right sides together, and machine stitch around the edges, leaving a 10" gap along one side. Turn the quilt right side out and sew the gap closed. Topstitch around the edges of the quilt. *See Figure 3.*

FIGURE 1

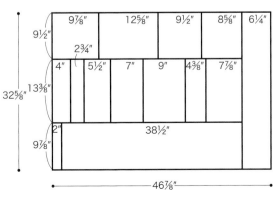

FIGURE 2

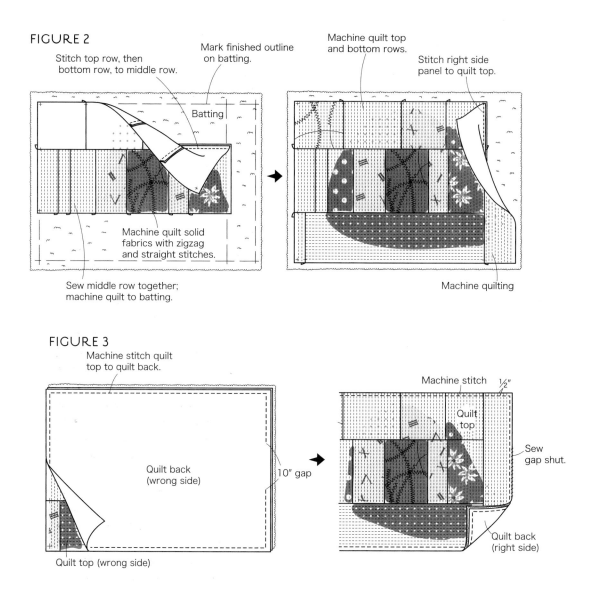

Stitch top row, then bottom row, to middle row.

Mark finished outline on batting.

Batting

Machine quilt top and bottom rows.

Stitch right side panel to quilt top.

Machine quilt solid fabrics with zigzag and straight stitches.

Sew middle row together; machine quilt to batting.

Machine quilting

FIGURE 3

Machine stitch quilt top to quilt back.

Machine stitch   ½"

Quilt top

Quilt back (wrong side)

10" gap

Sew gap shut.

Quilt top (wrong side)

Quilt back (right side)

POT HOLDERS

Photograph on pages 48–49

MATERIALS FOR POT HOLDER A (PAGE 48, LEFT)

- Fabric scraps for collage (solids, prints; the patterns and colors are up to you)
- Fabric for front and lining (linen): 11⅞" × 7⅞"
- Quilt batting: 17¾" × 7⅞"
- Ribbon: ¾" wide × 3" long

MATERIALS FOR POT HOLDER B (PAGE 48, RIGHT)

- Fabric scraps for collage (prints, velveteen; the patterns and colors are up to you)
- Fabric for front and lining (felt): 13¾" × 5⅝"
- Quilt batting: 13¾" × 5⅛"
- Hemp cord: 7½" long

MATERIALS FOR POT HOLDER C (PAGE 49, LEFT)

- Decorative patch (1)
- Fabric for front (felt): 5⅞" × 5⅞"
- Fabric for back (linen): 5⅞" × 5⅞"
- Quilt batting: 15¾" × 5⅞"
- Cotton thread (red)

MATERIALS FOR POT HOLDER D (PAGE 49, RIGHT)

- Fabric scraps for collage (prints, felt, ribbon; the patterns and colors are up to you)
- Fabric for front (felt): 7⅞" × 5⅞"
- Fabric for back (linen): 7⅞" × 5⅞"
- Quilt batting: 17¾" × 7⅞"
- Bias tape: ¼" wide × 4¾" long

INSTRUCTIONS

1. For all pot holders, place the top fabric on three layers of quilt batting. For pot holders A, B, and C, position fabric patches and stitch them to the top and batting layers according to the diagrams on page 122. Free stitch additional lines through all three layers according to the diagrams.

   For pot holder D, cut out the fabric flower pieces using the template on page 123. Place the flower on the top fabric and stitch around the outline of the flower to secure in place. For the flower center, cut a piece of felt and affix it using spiral stitches. Sew the ribbon and patches in place according to the diagram. *See Figure 1.*

2. For all pot holders, place the front piece on the back fabric, wrong sides together, and sew zigzag and straight stitches around the edges. Make the loops from the specified materials and sew them on as shown. *See Figure 2.*

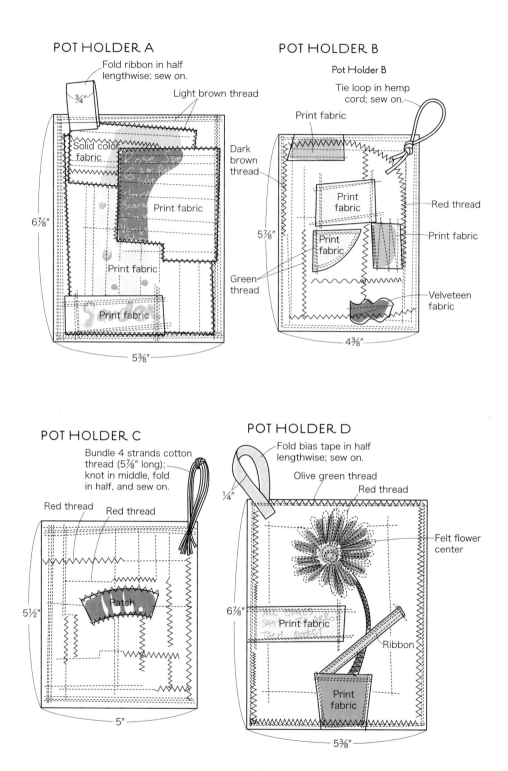

POT HOLDER A

Fold ribbon in half lengthwise; sew on.

¾"

Light brown thread

Solid color fabric

Print fabric

Dark brown thread

Print fabric

Print fabric

6⅞"

5⅜"

POT HOLDER B

Pot Holder B

Tie loop in hemp cord; sew on.

Print fabric

Print fabric

Print fabric

Red thread

Print fabric

5⅞"

Green thread

Velveteen fabric

4⅜"

POT HOLDER C

Bundle 4 strands cotton thread (5⅞" long); knot in middle, fold in half, and sew on.

Red thread   Red thread

Patch.

5½"

5"

POT HOLDER D

Fold bias tape in half lengthwise; sew on.

Olive green thread

Red thread

¼"

Felt flower center

6⅞"

Print fabric

Ribbon

Print fabric

5⅜"

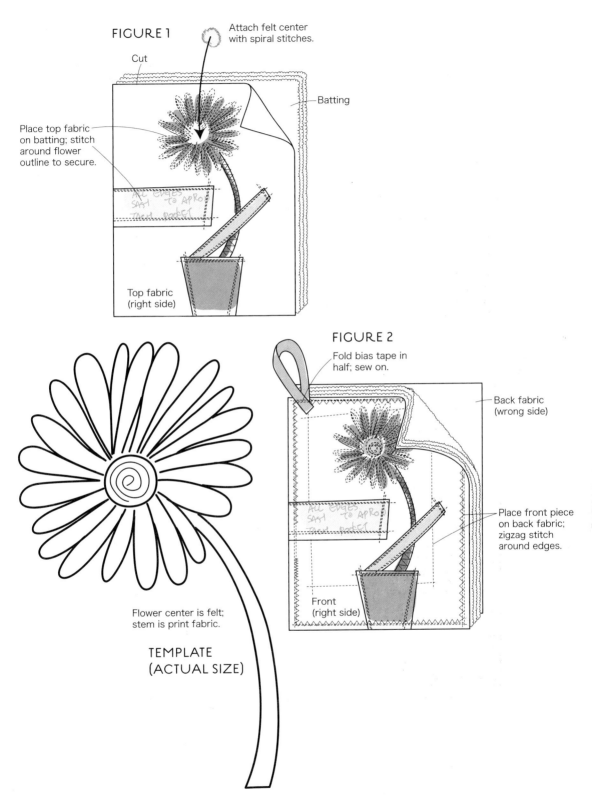

FIGURE 1

Cut

Attach felt center with spiral stitches.

Batting

Place top fabric on batting; stitch around flower outline to secure.

Top fabric (right side)

Flower center is felt; stem is print fabric.

TEMPLATE (ACTUAL SIZE)

FIGURE 2

Fold bias tape in half; sew on.

Back fabric (wrong side)

Place front piece on back fabric; zigzag stitch around edges.

Front (right side)

SHOULDER BAG

Photograph on pages 50–51

MATERIALS

- Fabric scraps for patchwork (white or off-white cotton, linen, silk, velvet; the colors and patterns are up to you)
- Fabric for front, back, and lining (linen): 19¾" × 17¾"
- Interior pocket (cotton): 7⅞" × 7⅞"
- Quilt batting: 19¾" × 11⅞"
- Sew-on, ready-made, leather handle (1): 3⁄16" wide × 18⅞" long
- Clasp (1)

FINISHED MEASUREMENTS

Add all seam allowances before cutting your fabric. *See Figure 1.*

INSTRUCTIONS

1. Mark a 7⅞" × 10¼" outline on the batting. Create the patchwork for the bag back on the batting one by one according to the diagram, layering pieces as you go and machine quilting each piece in place using both zigzag and straight stitches. Place some pieces face down to stitch in place and fold over, to create a clean seam; for other pieces, leave the raw edges exposed. Mark the finished outline again on the fabric and cut around it, leaving a seam allowance. *See Figure 2.*

2. Place the front exterior fabric on the batting and machine quilt the layers together with orange thread, making rows ⅝" apart. Position the fabric patch and sew it in place. Mark the finished outline on the fabric and cut around it, leaving a seam allowance. *See Figure 3.*

3. Make the interior pocket, following the instructions on page 71. Place the pocket on the right side of the lining fabric, approximately 5" from the top edge and sew in place along the sides and bottom. *See Figure 4.*

4. Place the bag back on the lining, right sides together; sew along the top and 3½" down each side to form the bag flap. Place the bag front on the lining, right sides together, and sew along the bottom edge. Fold open the bag front. Pull down the bag back so that it is on the bag front, right sides together; fold the lining in half on top of itself. Let the bag flap stand up, centered over the seam of the bag front and lining. Sew around the sides of the bag, leaving a 3" gap along one side. Turn the bag right side out through the lining and sew the gap closed. *See Figure 5.*

5. Sew half of the clasp to the right side of the flap. Close the flap to determine the position of the other half of the clasp; secure the other half to the bag front. Sew the leather handle to the sides of the bag. *See Figure 6.*

FIGURE 1

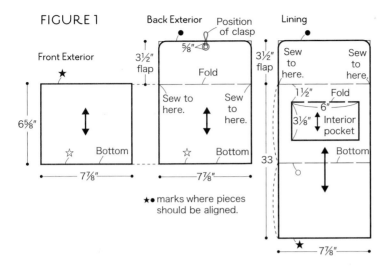

Front Exterior

★

6⅝"

Bottom
☆

7⅞"

Back Exterior

Position of clasp

⅝"

3½" flap

Fold

Sew to here.   Sew to here.

Bottom
☆

7⅞"

Lining

3½" flap

Sew to here.   Sew to here.

1½"   Fold

6"

3⅛"   Interior pocket

Bottom

33

★   7⅞"

★● marks where pieces should be aligned.

FIGURE 2

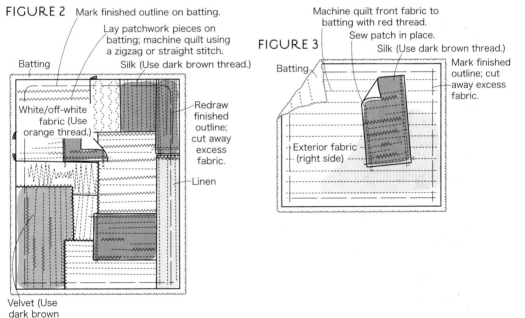

Mark finished outline on batting.

Lay patchwork pieces on batting; machine quilt using a zigzag or straight stitch.

Batting

Silk (Use dark brown thread.)

White/off-white fabric (Use orange thread.)

Redraw finished outline; cut away excess fabric.

Linen

Velvet (Use dark brown thread.)

FIGURE 3

Machine quilt front fabric to batting with red thread.

Sew patch in place.

Silk (Use dark brown thread.)

Mark finished outline; cut away excess fabric.

Batting

Exterior fabric (right side)

FIGURE 4

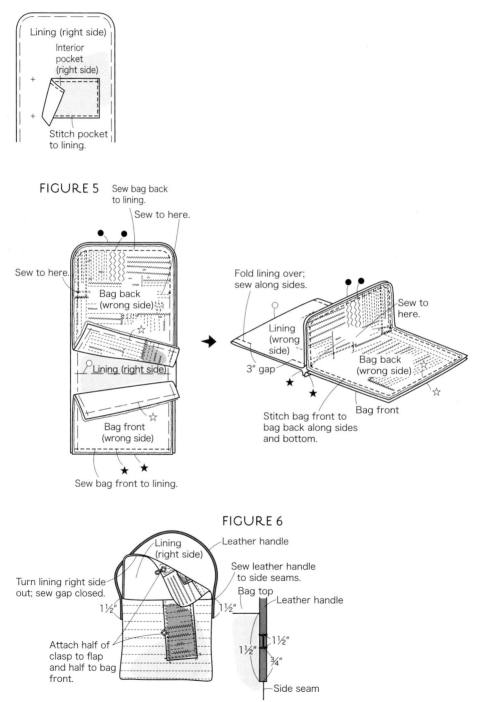

Lining (right side)

Interior pocket (right side)

Stitch pocket to lining.

FIGURE 5

Sew bag back to lining.

Sew to here.

Sew to here.

Bag back (wrong side)

Lining (right side)

Bag front (wrong side)

Sew bag front to lining.

Fold lining over; sew along sides.

Sew to here.

Lining (wrong side)

3" gap

Bag back (wrong side)

Bag front

Stitch bag front to bag back along sides and bottom.

FIGURE 6

Lining (right side)

Leather handle

Sew leather handle to side seams.

Bag top

Leather handle

Turn lining right side out; sew gap closed.

1½"

1½"

Attach half of clasp to flap and half to bag front.

1½"

¾"

Side seam

CURTAIN

Photograph on page 52

MATERIALS

- Fabric scraps for appliqués (22 different patterns)
- Ready-made curtain panel (check pattern with $4\frac{1}{4}$" × $4\frac{1}{4}$" squares): about $39\frac{3}{8}$" wide × $59\frac{1}{8}$" long

INSTRUCTIONS

1. Cut 22 pieces of appliqué fabric to $4\frac{3}{4}$" × $4\frac{3}{4}$" or a size determined by the curtain being used. Place a 4" × 4" piece of thick paper on the wrong side of the appliqué fabric, fold the seam allowance over the paper, and crease it with an iron; remove the paper. Arrange the appliqué squares on the curtain to create a balanced look and baste in place. Machine stitch around the edges of each square twice: $\frac{1}{16}$" from edge and $\frac{1}{4}$" from edge. Machine quilt an X through each appliqué square. *See Figure 1.*

FIGURE 1

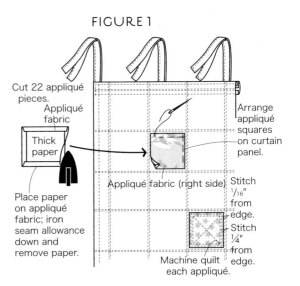

Cut 22 appliqué pieces.

Appliqué fabric

Thick paper

Place paper on appliqué fabric; iron seam allowance down and remove paper.

Arrange appliqué squares on curtain panel.

Appliqué fabric (right side)

Stitch $\frac{1}{16}$" from edge.

Stitch $\frac{1}{4}$" from edge.

Machine quilt each appliqué.

TOTE BAG

Photograph on page 53

MATERIALS

- Fabric scraps for appliqués (prints; the patterns and colors are up to you)
- Exterior fabric (linen): 27½" × 15¾"
- Lining (cotton print): 21⅜" × 27½"
- Fusible interfacing for exterior fabric: 27½" × 15¾"
- Double-sided fusible interfacing for appliqués: 9⅞" × 7⅞"
- Ready-made leather handles with metal clips (2): 16½" long

FINISHED MEASUREMENTS

Add all seam allowances before cutting your fabric. *See Figure 1.*

INSTRUCTIONS

1. Apply fusible interfacing to the wrong side of the bag front. Machine stitch a grid (4 squares by 4 squares) on the bag front for the appliqués. Apply double-sided fusible interfacing to the wrong side of the appliqué squares. Remove the backing paper and iron the appliqués onto the bag front, according to the manufacturer's instructions. (See also the appliqué instructions on page 79.) Sew each square in place with zigzag stitches; machine quilt an X through all or some of the appliqués. *See Figure 2.*

2. Apply fusible interfacing to the wrong side of the bag back. Using the template on page 123 as a guide, cut out the appliqué and apply adhesive backing to the wrong side. Remove the backing paper and iron the appliqué onto the bag back according to the manufacturer's instructions. Sew in place with free motion stitching. *See Figure 3.*

3. Place the bag front on the bag back, right sides together, and sew around the sides and bottom. Press the seams open. *See Figure 4.*

4. Fold the pocket fabric in half, right sides together, and sew around the three open sides, leaving a 2¾" gap along the bottom. Turn the pocket right side out, sew the gap closed, and attach it to the lining, approximately 2⅜" from the top edge. Fold the lining in half, right sides together, and stitch along the bottom and both sides, leaving a gap approximately 4¾" long in the side seam. *See Figure 5.*

5. Place the bag lining over the bag exterior, right sides together, and stitch around the bag top. Press the seam allowances to one side. Turn the bag right side out; sew the gap in the lining closed. Attach the handles to the bag top. *See Figure 6.*

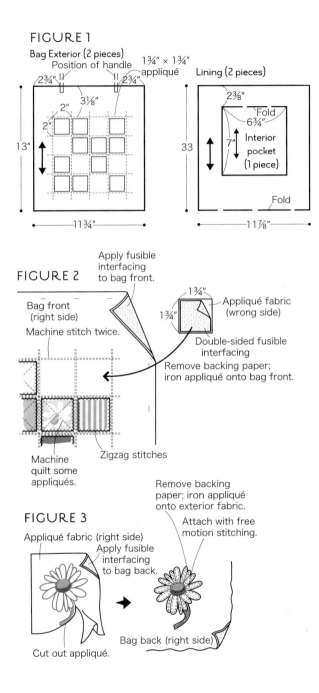

FIGURE 1

Bag Exterior (2 pieces)
Position of handle
1¾" × 1¾" appliqué
Lining (2 pieces)

2¾" | | | | 2¾"
3⅛"
2"
2"
13"
11¾"

2⅜"
Fold
6¾"
7"
Interior pocket (1 piece)
33
Fold
11⅞"

FIGURE 2

Apply fusible interfacing to bag front.

Bag front (right side)
Machine stitch twice.

1¾"
1¾"
Appliqué fabric (wrong side)
Double-sided fusible interfacing
Remove backing paper; iron appliqué onto bag front.

Machine quilt some appliqués.
Zigzag stitches

FIGURE 3

Appliqué fabric (right side)
Apply fusible interfacing to bag back.

Remove backing paper; iron appliqué onto exterior fabric.
Attach with free motion stitching.

Cut out appliqué.
Bag back (right side)

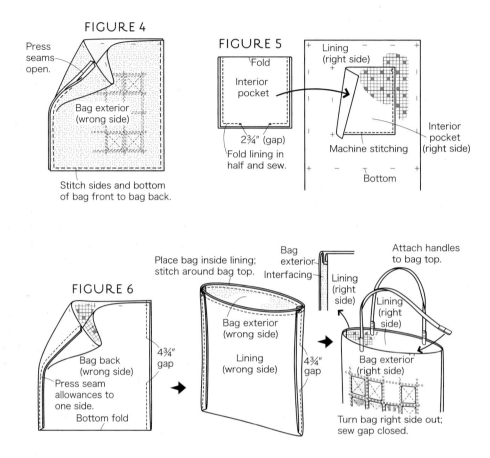

FIGURE 4

Press seams open.

Bag exterior (wrong side)

Stitch sides and bottom of bag front to bag back.

FIGURE 5

Fold

Interior pocket

2¾" (gap)

Fold lining in half and sew.

Lining (right side)

Machine stitching

Interior pocket (right side)

Bottom

FIGURE 6

Bag back (wrong side)

Press seam allowances to one side.

Bottom fold

4¾" gap

Place bag inside lining; stitch around bag top.

Bag exterior

Interfacing

Bag exterior (wrong side)

Lining (wrong side)

4¾" gap

Attach handles to bag top.

Lining (right side)

Lining (right side)

Bag exterior (right side)

Turn bag right side out; sew gap closed.

FOLDED POT HOLDERS

Photograph on page 54

MATERIALS FOR THE POT HOLDER ON THE LEFT

· Clothing labels for collage (7 different types)
· Fabric for front (solid color and polka dots): 3½" × 8" each
· Fabric for back (print): 6" × 8"
· Quilt batting: 17¾" × 8"

MATERIALS FOR THE POT HOLDER ON THE RIGHT

· Fabric scraps for collage (solid colors, prints; the colors and patterns are up to you)
· Fabric for back (wool): 6" × 10"
· Fabric for binding (polka dots): 12" × 12" *or* bias tape (double fold): ¼" × 15"
· Fabric for binding (solid color): 6" × 6" *or* bias tape (double fold): ¼" × 5"
· Quilt batting: 17¾" × 10"
· Ribbon: ⅜" wide × 10" long

FINISHED MEASUREMENTS

Add all seam allowances before cutting your fabric. *See Figure 1.*

INSTRUCTIONS

1. For the pot holder on the left, place the two pieces of fabric for the front right sides together on three layers of batting; align the edges and sew along one edge. Open the fabric and attach the clothing labels to the front fabric as a collage.

For the pot holder on the right, place three layers of batting together; mark the finished outline on top. Using the template on page 132. Sew the fabric scraps directly to the batting, layering the fabrics together as you like to make a collage.

For both pot holders, machine quilt the entire surface, making rows ⅜" apart. Mark the finished outline on the fabric and stitch just inside the finished outline, about ¹⁄₁₆" from the edge; cut around the outline, leaving a seam allowance. *See Figure 2.*

2. For the pot holder on the left, place the front fabric on the back fabric, right sides together. Stitch around all four sides, leaving a 3" gap along one side. Turn the pot holder right side out and sew the gap closed.

For the pot holder on the right, place the front fabric on the back fabric, wrong sides together. Take a piece of fabric 1" wide for the binding and press the long edges to the center. Open up the fabric and align the raw edge of the binding with the raw edge of the pot holder, right sides together. Stitch the binding in place in the fold, alternating between the solid color and checks, around all sides on the front. Tie a loop with a single knot in one end of the ribbon. Place the ribbon across the center of the pot holder back; align one end with the side of the pot holder. Sew the ribbon in place across the back of the pot holder. Fold the binding to the back and hand stitch in place. *See Figure 3.*

FIGURE 1

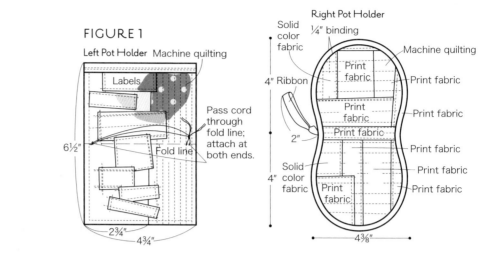

Left Pot Holder — Machine quilting

Labels

6½"

Pass cord through fold line; attach at both ends.

Fold line

2¾"

4¾"

Right Pot Holder

Solid color fabric

¼" binding

Machine quilting

4" Ribbon

Print fabric

Print fabric

Print fabric

2"

Print fabric

Print fabric

Print fabric

Print fabric

Solid color fabric

4" Print fabric

4⅜"

FIGURE 2

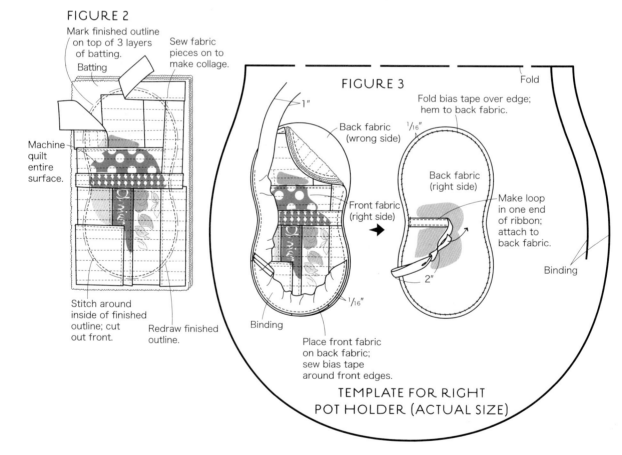

Mark finished outline on top of 3 layers of batting.

Batting

Sew fabric pieces on to make collage.

Machine quilt entire surface.

Stitch around inside of finished outline; cut out front.

Redraw finished outline.

FIGURE 3

1"

Fold

Fold bias tape over edge; hem to back fabric.

1/16"

Back fabric (wrong side)

Back fabric (right side)

Front fabric (right side)

Make loop in one end of ribbon; attach to back fabric.

2"

Binding

Binding

1/16"

Place front fabric on back fabric; sew bias tape around front edges.

TEMPLATE FOR RIGHT POT HOLDER (ACTUAL SIZE)

POT HOLDERS

Photograph on page 55

MATERIALS FOR THE POT HOLDER ON THE LEFT

· Fabric scraps for collage (prints, velvet; the patterns and colors are up to you)
· Top fabric (linen): 8" × 8"
· Bottom fabric (thick wool): 8" × 8"
· Quilt batting: 24" × 8"
· Hemp cord: 18¾"

MATERIALS FOR THE POT HOLDER IN THE CENTER

· Fabric scraps for collage (prints, wool, cloth labels; the colors and patterns are up to you)
· Top fabric (linen): 8" × 8"
· Bottom fabric (heavy cotton): 8" × 8"
· Quilt batting: 24" × 8"
· Ribbon: ¾" wide × 3½" long

MATERIALS FOR THE POT HOLDER ON THE RIGHT

· Fabric scraps for collage (prints; the colors and patterns are up to you)
· Top fabric (solid color): 8" × 8"
· Bottom fabric (stripes): 8" × 8"
· Quilt batting: 24" × 8"
· Hemp cord: 19¾"

FINISHED MEASUREMENTS

Add all seam allowances before cutting your fabric. *See Figure 1.*

INSTRUCTIONS

1. Place the front fabric on top of three layers of quilt batting. Lay out the fabric pieces for the collage on the front fabric, and sew them in place. Machine quilt the entire surface, making rows ¼" apart. Mark the finished outline and trim away excess fabric, leaving a seam allowance.

   Determine the type and placement of the hemp loops or tab according to the diagrams on page 134. Baste the ends to right side of the pot holder front, just outside the finished outline. *See Figure 2.*

2. Place the front fabric on the back fabric, right sides together, and stitch the edges together, leaving a 2¾" opening in one side. Turn the pot holder right side out and sew the gap closed. Top-stitch around all four sides. *See Figure 3.*

FIGURE 1

Pot Holder on the Left

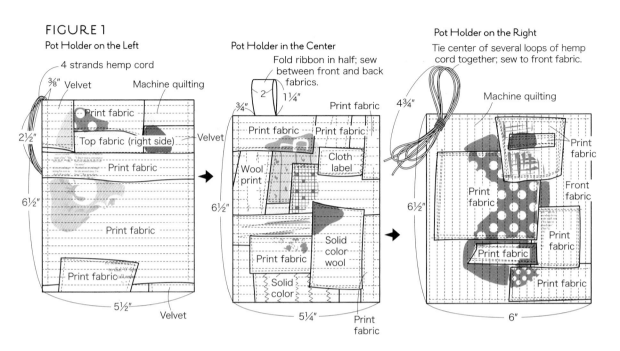

4 strands hemp cord

⅜" Velvet

Machine quilting

Print fabric

Top fabric (right side)

Velvet

Print fabric

2½"

6½"

Print fabric

Print fabric

5½"

Velvet

Pot Holder in the Center

Fold ribbon in half; sew between front and back fabrics.

2

1¼"

¾"

Print fabric

Print fabric

Print fabric

Cloth label

Wool print

6½"

Solid color wool

Print fabric

Print fabric

Solid color

5¼"

Print fabric

Pot Holder on the Right

Tie center of several loops of hemp cord together; sew to front fabric.

4¾"

Machine quilting

Print fabric

Front fabric

Print fabric

6½"

Print fabric

Print fabric

Print fabric

6"

FIGURE 2

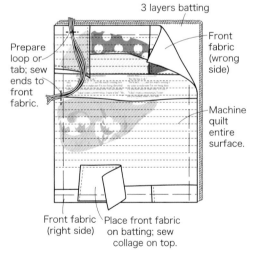

3 layers batting

Prepare loop or tab; sew ends to front fabric.

Front fabric (wrong side)

Machine quilt entire surface.

Front fabric (right side)

Place front fabric on batting; sew collage on top.

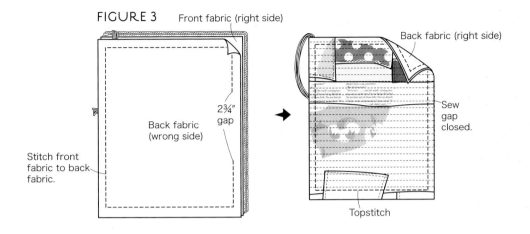

FIGURE 3   Front fabric (right side)

Back fabric (wrong side)

2¾" gap

Stitch front fabric to back fabric.

Back fabric (right side)

Sew gap closed.

Topstitch

POCKET TISSUE CASE

Photograph on page 56

MATERIALS

- Fabric scraps for collage and patchwork (prints, stripes, etc.; the colors and patterns are up to you)
- Fabric for exterior and lining (linen): 27½" × 6"
- Zipper (1): 5" long
- Quilt batting: 7" × 6"

FINISHED MEASUREMENTS

Add all seam allowances before cutting your fabric. *See Figure 1.*

INSTRUCTIONS

1. Place the two pieces for the pouch front right sides together; stitch two lines in the center of the fabric from the edge to ½" inside the finished outline to form the tissue opening. Turn the fabric right side out, folding each piece in half along the stitch lines; backstitch across both ends of the tissue opening. Make a col-lage of fabric scraps and stitch them to the front fabric. *See Figure 2.*

2. For the back of the tissue pouch, make a log cabin, following the instructions on page 62. *See Figure 3.*

3. Place the pouch front on the zipper between the two layers, right sides together. Align the edge of the zipper tape with the edge of the front fabric; sew along the edge. Fold the front fabric back. Place the pouch back on the other side of the zipper, right sides together; place the lining on the wrong side of the zipper. Align the edges and sew through all three layers. Fold the back fabric and lining back; machine quilt the pouch back, making rows ¼" apart. *See Figure 4.*

4. Open the zipper. Place the pouch front on the pouch back, right sides together, and sew around the sides, rounding the corners as you sew. Turn the pouch right side out through the zipper. *See Figure 5.*

FIGURE 1

Pouch Front

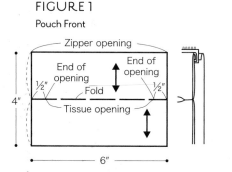

Pouch Back and Lining (1 piece each)

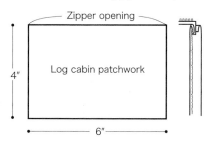

FIGURE 2

Place two pouch front pieces together; stitch from outside edges to ends of tissue opening.

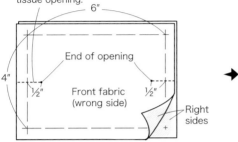

6"

End of opening

4"

½"   Front fabric
(wrong side)   ½"

Right sides

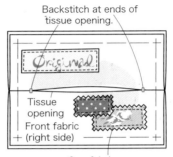

Backstitch at ends of tissue opening.

Original

Tissue opening
Front fabric
(right side)

Sew fabric scraps to make collage on front fabric.

FIGURE 3

Sew fabric strips to batting to make log cabin.

Batting

FIGURE 4

Pouch front
(wrong side)

Zipper
(right side)

⅜"

Place pouch front on zipper; sew in place.

Zipper
(right side)

Pouch front
(right side)

Pouch back

Machine quilt through all layers.

Lining
(wrong side)

Pouch back
(right side)

Layer zipper between pouch back and lining; sew in place.

Pouch front
(right side)

FIGURE 5

Open zipper.

Zigzag stitches

Zigzag stitches

Round corner seams.

Back lining
(right side)

Sew pouch front to pouch back.

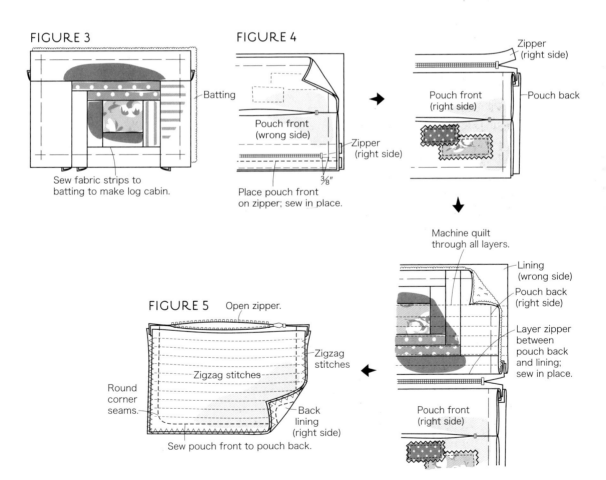

APRON

Photograph on page 57

MATERIALS

- Fabric scraps for collage (prints; the patterns and colors are up to you)
- Fabric for exterior and main pocket (linen): $31\frac{1}{2}$" × $37\frac{3}{8}$"
- Fabric for ties (cotton, solid color): $41\frac{1}{2}$" × 4"
- Fabric for pocket lining (cotton, stripes): $31\frac{1}{2}$" × $7\frac{7}{8}$"
- Fabric for pocket backing (thin cotton): $31\frac{1}{2}$" × $7\frac{7}{8}$"
- Quilt batting: $31\frac{1}{2}$" × $7\frac{7}{8}$"

FINISHED MEASUREMENTS

Add all seam allowances before cutting your fabric. *See Figure 1.*

INSTRUCTIONS

1. Lay the fabric for the main pocket on top of the batting and backing. Mark the placement of the pocket divisions. Arrange the fabric pieces for the collage on top, and sew them in place one at a time. Machine quilt the entire main pocket in vertical rows $\frac{3}{8}$" apart (being sure to not quilt over the pocket divisions).

   Use a large piece of print fabric (this size is up to you) for a smaller pocket. Fold the top edge under twice and stitch. Place the smaller pocket on the main pocket and sew along the bottom and both sides, leaving the raw edges exposed.

   Place the main pocket on the lining, right sides together, and sew along the top edge. Turn it right side out. *See Figure 2.*

2. Place the main pocket on the apron front, right side up. Align along the bottom edge and sides and baste in place. Place the apron back on the apron front, right sides together, and sew around all four sides, leaving a 8" gap along the top edge. Turn the apron right side out and sew the gap closed. *See Figure 3.*

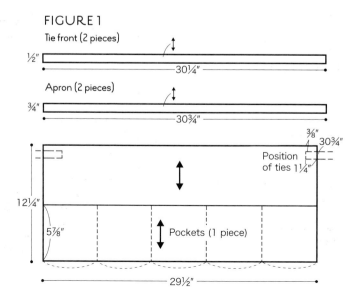

FIGURE 1

Tie front (2 pieces)

$\frac{1}{2}$"

30$\frac{1}{4}$"

Apron (2 pieces)

$\frac{3}{4}$"

30$\frac{3}{4}$"

$\frac{3}{8}$"
30$\frac{3}{4}$"
Position of ties 1$\frac{1}{4}$"

12$\frac{1}{4}$"

5$\frac{7}{8}$"

Pockets (1 piece)

29$\frac{1}{2}$"

4. Fold the long edges of the four ties to the center. Place the tie back on the tie front, wrong sides together, and stitch along both long edges. Place the ties on either side of the apron front, 1" from the outside edge. Sew the tie in place, stitching a square and then diagonally through the square. Sew along the division lines on the pocket. *See Figure 4.*

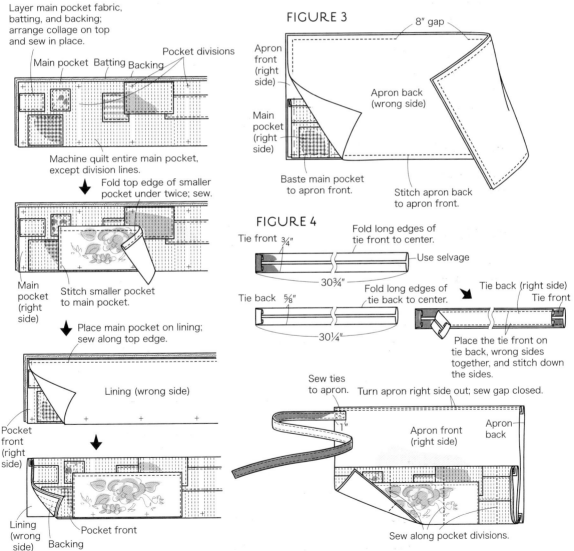

FIGURE 2

Layer main pocket fabric, batting, and backing; arrange collage on top and sew in place.

Main pocket   Batting   Backing

Pocket divisions

Machine quilt entire main pocket, except division lines.

Fold top edge of smaller pocket under twice; sew.

Main pocket (right side)

Stitch smaller pocket to main pocket.

Place main pocket on lining; sew along top edge.

Lining (wrong side)

Pocket front (right side)

Lining (wrong side)   Backing   Pocket front

FIGURE 3

8" gap

Apron front (right side)

Apron back (wrong side)

Main pocket (right side)

Baste main pocket to apron front.

Stitch apron back to apron front.

FIGURE 4

Tie front 3/4"

Fold long edges of tie front to center.

Use selvage

30 3/4"

Tie back 5/8"

Fold long edges of tie back to center.

30 1/4"

Tie back (right side)   Tie front

Place the tie front on tie back, wrong sides together, and stitch down the sides.

Sew ties to apron.   Turn apron right side out; sew gap closed.

1"

Apron front (right side)

Apron back

Sew along pocket divisions.

FLOOR MAT

Photograph on page 58

MATERIALS

- Fabric scraps for collage (prints; the colors and patterns are up to you)
- Foundation cloth (linen): $35\frac{1}{2}$" × $23\frac{1}{2}$"
- Back (cotton, stripes): $31\frac{1}{2}$" × 43"
- Quilt batting: $35\frac{1}{2}$" × $47\frac{1}{4}$"

FINISHED MEASUREMENTS

Add all seam allowances before cutting your fabric. *See Figure 1.*

INSTRUCTIONS

1. Baste the foundation cloth to a piece of batting of the same dimensions. Sew the fabric scraps to the foundation cloth one by one according to the diagram, layering pieces as you go. Place some pieces face down to stitch in place and fold over, to create a clean seam; for other pieces, leave the raw edges exposed. Machine stitch each collage piece to the foundation cloth one at a time: machine quilt the larger pieces horizontally, making rows $1\frac{1}{2}$" apart; machine quilt the smaller pieces vertically, making rows $\frac{3}{8}$" apart. *See Figure 2.*

2. Add one more layer of batting to the machine-quilted top. Lay the mat top right side up on the back so there is $2\frac{3}{4}$" of the back fabric showing on all sides. Baste the layers together vertically, horizontally, and at the corners. Fold the back fabric twice toward the mat top to create a border $1\frac{3}{8}$" wide (cut the fabric if necessary). The mat back should overlap the mat top by $1\frac{3}{8}$". Stitch along the inside and outside edges of the border. *See Figure 3.*

FIGURE 1

Mat

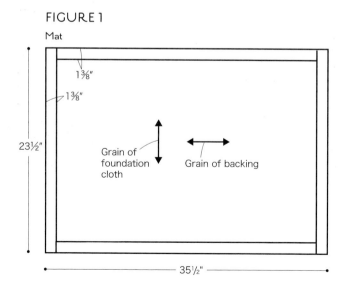

$1\frac{3}{8}$"

$1\frac{3}{8}$"

$23\frac{1}{2}$"

Grain of foundation cloth

Grain of backing

$35\frac{1}{2}$"

FIGURE 2

Baste foundation cloth to batting.

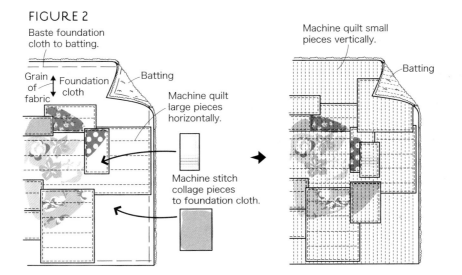

Grain of fabric

Foundation cloth

Batting

Machine quilt large pieces horizontally.

Machine stitch collage pieces to foundation cloth.

Machine quilt small pieces vertically.

Batting

FIGURE 3

Grain of fabric

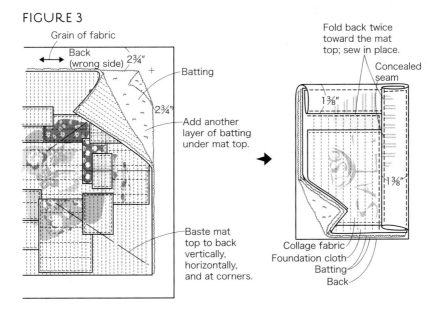

Back (wrong side)

2¾"

Batting

2¾"

Add another layer of batting under mat top.

Baste mat top to back vertically, horizontally, and at corners.

Fold back twice toward the mat top; sew in place.

Concealed seam

1⅜"

1⅜"

Collage fabric
Foundation cloth
Batting
Back

RESOURCES

The fabrics and notions used throughout this book were supplied from Japanese retailers, which you will find listed below. Since you may be unable to shop in Japan, retailers based in the United States and the United Kingdom are also provided, though they may not carry the exact materials found in this book.

BE IN (QUILT LOVERS)
Miyazaki Building 2F
Jingumae 6-28-5
Shibuya-ku
Tokyo, Japan
+81-3-3498-6308

FABRIC DEPOT
700 SE 122nd Ave
Portland, OR 97233
(503) 252-6267
www.Fabricdepot.com

GRAYLINE LINEN
260 West 39th Street
New York, NY 10018
(212) 391-4130
www.Graylinelinen.com

PURL PATCHWORK
147 Sullivan Street
New York, NY 10012
(212) 420-8798
www.Purlsoho.com

REPRODEPOT FABRICS
(413) 527-4047
www.Reprodepot.com
Online retailer based in Easthampton, Mass.

TALL POPPY CRAFT
(212) 813-3223
www.Tallpoppycraft.com
Online retailer based in New York City.

U-HANDBAG
+44 0-208-3103612
www.U-handbag.com
Online retailer based in London.

YUWA SHOTEN
Funagoshi-cho 1-5-4
Chuo-ku
Osaka, Japan
+81-6-6947-6777

ABOUT THE AUTHOR

Suzuko Koseki teaches at the Heart and Hands Patchwork School, the Asahi Cultural Center in Tachikawa, and the Vogue Quilt Institute in Japan.

Trumpeter Books
An imprint of Shambhala Publications, Inc.
Horticultural Hall
300 Massachusetts Avenue
Boston, Massachusetts 02115
www.shambhala.com

Originally published as *Mishin dakara tanoshiino* by Suzuko Kozeki

© 2004 by Suzuko Koseki

Originally published in Japan in 2004 by Bunka Publishing Bureau, Tokyo
World English translation rights arranged with Bunka Publishing Bureau through The English
Agency (Japan) Ltd.

Translation © 2008 by Shambhala Publications, Inc.

9 8 7 6 5 4 3 2

Printed in China

♾ This edition is printed on acid-free paper that meets the American National Standards
Institute Z39.48 Standard.
♻ Shambhala Publications makes every effort to print on recycled paper.
For more information please visit www.shambhala.com.

Distributed in the United States by Random House, Inc.,
and in Canada by Random House of Canada Ltd

Library of Congress Cataloging-in-Publication Data
Koseki, Suzuko.
[Mishin dakara tanoshiino. English]
Patchwork style: 35 simple projects for a cozy and colorful life / Suzuko Koseki.
p.   cm.— (Make good: Crafts + life)
ISBN 978-1-59030-649-9 (pbk.: alk. paper)
1. Patchwork—Patterns. 2. Quilting—Patterns. I. Title.
TT835.K67 2009
746.46'041—dc22
2008032339